CAIRNGORMS SCENE
AND UNSEEN

Sydney Scroggie. Photo by kind permission of Scottish Television.

THE
CAIRNGORMS SCENE
AND UNSEEN

by

SYDNEY SCROGGIE

With 9 photographic illustrations by Tom Weir and
12 line drawings by John Mitchell

SCOTTISH MOUNTAINEERING TRUST

First published in 1989 by The Scottish Mountaineering Trust
Copyright © by Sydney Scroggie

British Library Cataloguing in Publication Data
Scroggie, Sydney
    The cairngorms scene - and unseen.
    1. Mountaineering. Scroggie, Sydney
    I. Title
    796.5'22'0924

    ISBN 0-907521-25-8

Origination by Arneg, Glasgow
Typeset by Bureau-Graphics Ltd, Glasgow
Printed by Pillans & Wilson, Edinburgh
Bound by Hunter & Foulis, Edinburgh

LIST OF ILLUSTRATIONS

FOREWORD BY TOM WEIR

Here was an advertisement that stirred excitement when it arrived for publication in a Dundee newspaper in the winter of 1958:

> Blind hill man, due to senescence,
> indolence, hibernation,or house
> arrest of friends, requires patient,
> hardy companion for Clova weekend.
> Abominable snowman (tent trained)
> admirably suited, but no guide
> dogs need apply. Accommodation
> cramped; conditions appalling,
> hours endless, wages nil..........

The advert never reached the public. But one in the office who had read it, Bob McLean, followed it up, and it wasn't a hoax. Sydney Scroggie really was looking for a companion who would act as a pair of eyes for him. Bob McLean discovered what had not been disclosed to him until the tent was down and he was rummaging about for something suitable to make a pillow. "Try this," said Syd, and passed him across the wooden leg he had just taken off.

Scroggie was soon to become something of a legend among outdoor folk, a blind Dundonian who wore the kilt, and on any reasonably warm day walked to work with his shirt off to enjoy the sunshine on his bare back. Although I hadn't met him, I felt I knew him from his book of verses full of imagery of his delight in the great outdoors. Here is a sample:

> Sun on the bothy, wind on the grass
> Shadow of cumulus over the pass:
> Yawning and scratching and stretching of legs,
> Boiling the billy and frying the eggs.
>
> Moon on the loch, a bouldery camp,
> Guy-ropes like banjo-strings, matchboxes damp;
> The primus is bust, the pricker is bent,
> But there's baccy and whisky galore in the tent.
>
> An easterly wind, a bedraggling mist,
> Rainwater trickling in at the wrist,
> Wet to the belly, wet to the bum,
> The boots are awash and the fingers are numb.

A furnace of sun, a tropical day,
Drowsy the hills across the way;
Line dangles listlessly over the edge
And the third man's asleep on a heathery ledge.

Dazzling cornice, pink cirrus or two,
Ice-crystals sparkling up in the blue;
One more Goldflake and the bastard will go
And the fragments are dancing and tinkling below.

What I did not realise was that Sydney was blinded at 25 years of age, and that that lively poem was written over 30 years later, yet the inner vision had the brightness of immediacy. I discovered this was not only true about the poems but about the man, when I went to the Cairngorms with him and got him to talk to me about his life, for a television programme.

After it was shown, all sorts of stories about Syd reached me from folk who had crossed his path in the army and out of it. One of the most interesting letters came from May Macfarlane of Kilbarchan who was at his bedside shortly after Syd was blinded in action in Italy a fortnight before the war ended. She wrote:

"Let me relate the encounter, still crystal clear after forty years. I was a patient in Naples Military Hospital, and heard there was a Scot in the blind ward. It was Syd Scroggie though I didn't know his name until years later.

"Despite the gravity of his condition he explained bluntly, 'Stood on a mine - light, then darkness. I can live without my sight, but never without my mountains.'

'Which mountains ?' I asked.
'What would you know about mountains ?'
'Well, I've stayed in Corrour bothy.'

"This led to talk of the Cairngorms, Glencoe and the Arrochar peaks. When the Sister signalled me to withdraw, Syd's parting shot was, 'Well, there's a V.E. party tomorrow - enjoy your victory cake.'

"I returned to the blind ward and shared the cake with Syd. The next day he was aboard a hospital ship bound for home; I was on a launch for Sorrento and convalescence. We did not exchange names.

"Twenty years later, in Montreal, I was given a batch of Scots Magazines, one of which, dated November 1965, had an article entitled "Syd Scroggie - Man of the Hills". On reading it I concluded that it had to be my victory cake warrior. I dropped a line to Syd, and the nub of the reply was, 'I remember a faint you, but was under sedation. Do write more.'

"A visit was arranged and meeting him was a momentous occasion. Since retirement Syd's name has cropped up from time to time. There is his book of verse, copies of which I have passed to mountain-loving friends; and what I thought of his courage in Naples I think so today. If you are in touch with Syd, please convey my best wishes to him and his very supportive wife and family."

I passed on the message when I visited him at his cottage in Strathmartine just north of Dundee. Expecting me, he was already rigged for the hills, and all he had to do was pick up the long staff he uses to compensate for his wooden leg. A riveting talker, he was soon launched on a description of a climb he'd just done with Margaret whom he married following the death of his first wife in 1980.

"We were at 2,500 feet, weren't we Margaret," he said with appreciation "and white hares were running, there was a herd of red deer, aye, and a ptarmigan flying; great sights !" He spoke with the feeling of one who had seen them, as indeed he had, through Margaret's eyes.

It took him ten years of learning how to cope with infirmity before he was ready to set out with week-end kit in his rucksack for Corrour bothy in the Lairig Ghru, and it sparked off one of his best poems which appears in this autobiographical tale, where sometimes it is hard to tell what is fact and what is fantasy. When I said that to him, he replied, "True enough, for in time fantasy takes over and the memory is maybe better for that. It's not details that count."

The book enchanted me because of the gradual and humorous way he unfolds his tale with an art that conceals art. Because it is not chronological he keeps you guessing but does not forget to satisfy your curiosity when the time is ripe. Any man he meets or climbs with is not just a name, but is given dimension by juicy bits of conversation and flash-backs into the history of the person. I'd rather have this novelistic approach than a detailed list of the 600 blind climbs he had done covering thousands of miles on the hills.

We go beyond topography here into the realm of eternal truths about man and mountain, not forgetting women, nor the overwhelming effect of the hills on the mind of a solitary person. One of the best chapters is about his own son, Jamie, who suddenly discovered what irrational fear was, in the Lairig Ghru.

Summit Ben Macdhui

In the Cairngorms, Ben Macdhui has the reputation of being haunted by a Big Grey Man, claimed to have been seen by the Scottish pioneer of Himalayan climbing, Dr. A. M. Kellas, who had done more high-altitude climbing than anyone alive, but died of heart-failure in 1921 on the first ever attempt on Mount Everest.

It was another world famous mountaineer at the beginning of the century who next encountered something beyond his understanding, Professor Norman Collie, a Fellow of the Royal Society and native of Aberdeenshire. As he walked on the gravelly summit, he heard crunching sounds out of sympathy with his own, as if someone was following and taking bigger steps. In the mist he could see nothing, but still the crunch, crunch sounded behind him as he walked on. Reasoning suddenly gave way to terror: "I took to my heels, staggering blindly among the boulders for four or five miles nearly down to Rothiemurchus Forest." His last words were: "There is something very queer about the top of Ben Macdhui and I will not go back there myself, I know."

To give Syd's narrative shape I had to make some savage cuts. The trunk of the story had too many diverting branches. When I said so to Syd, he said "Any bit of writing can be improved by shortening, and that's true of most bits of writing. I give you carte blanche." One tale I did cut out is about Jimmy Stewart, but this is it in shortened version.

Jimmy was a bachelor, an Atholl man, the son of a Glen Tilt keeper, a hill shepherd who had served in the Lovat Scouts with Syd, and was known to his fellow squaddies by the name of the house where he shepherded, "Shinagag". In his manuscript Syd had described this character as

"...a cheerful personality of bawling voice and rough and ready hospitality, his red face, bald head and single tobacco-stained tooth, his dog, pipe, whisky bottle, lambing stick and unbuckled boots, a byword for worthiness."

The motto of the Lovat Scouts is "Je suis pret" (I am ready), and Syd in his wartime days with Jimmy had combined this motto with him in skittish verses. This is one of them:

> Think of the black and white
> bonnet
> The buckled belt with the stag's
> head on it;
> Ready were you and ready I,
> Ready to scrounge and dodge
> and lie,
> Ready a soldier's death to die,
> Shinagag.

One day in Glen Tilt, and turning up for Loch Moraig, two of us decided to take the ancient drove road to Kirkmichael and visit this lonely house which we had heard now lay empty. Following a rough track, the same used by Mary Queen of Scots in 1564 when she attended a famous deer hunt as guest of the Earl of Atholl, we were on the slopes of a Beinn a' Ghlo where 2000 deer were driven to the hunters.

From the 1400 feet level, suddenly Shinagag stood distantly before us, the slopes below the house dotted with sheep and cattle grazing on each side of green Glen Girnaig. As we walked to it I was picturing a meeting between old friends here in the bitter winter of 1963 when Syd and a companion had forced a way over 22 feet snowdrifts to surprise Jimmy Stewart, and great joy it gave him, for the house had been cut off from Glen Tilt since November, and Syd had brought some whisky with him, little knowing that he was going to be Jimmy's "first foot". The date for that Hogmanay celebration was February 23rd.

Phoning Syd to tell him about my walk to Shinagag I asked him about Jimmy, wondering where he was now. The answer struck like a blow. "He's dead. He was murdered. He had taken a job in the wilds of Glen Lyon, and was found dying, face-down with a hole in his head. He never regained consciousness. The official inquest called it "accidental death", perhaps the result of a fall. But quite a number of folk think the same as I do, that he was clubbed to death by a marauder. The whole thing is a mystery."

Jimmy Stewart, born on Armistice day 1918, had survived hard fighting in Italy to die in what is sometimes called the glen of the three "L's", the longest, the loneliest and the loveliest glen in Scotland, in a house you would have thought no harm could have befallen him.

As for Syd, he had his closest call to death in the Cairngorms not so very long ago. I leave him to tell you the tale in his own inimitable fashion.

CHAPTER ONE

The Pools of Dee, Lairig Ghru

It was scorching, in fact I don't think two people ever traversed the long pass from the forest of Rothiemurchus to Luibeg under a clearer sky and hotter sun than Bob and I did that May day in 1959. The pines of Speyside were drenched in early morning dew as we made our way from Aviemore and up the stony track to the crossing of the Allt Druie. Cuckoos called, and already the rising sun was dazzling where it glanced between dark needles and gnarled limbs. We reached the top of the Lairig Ghru, the great pass through the Cairngorms, in the full heat of the day. Just over the crest there was water, the ice-cold Pools of Dee. The curly bearded McLean flung off his clothes, gave a whoop which echoed off the enclosing red walls of the pass and hurled himself into the biggest of the pools.

He did not stay long in the water, but scrambled out immediately on to a patch of spiky grass, moss and small stones where his sweat-sodden shirt and breeks lay drying in the sun. He was trying to get his breath back, and his bearing was that of a man who has just come through a frightful ordeal from which it will take time to recover.

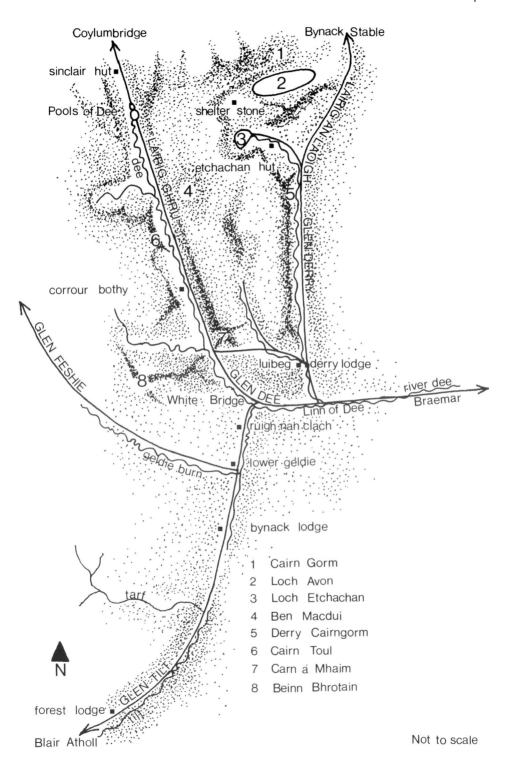

Coylumbridge

Bynack Stable

sinclair hut ■

Pools of Dee

shelter stone ■

1

2

LAIRIG AN LAOIGH

etchachan hut

3 ■

4

5

dee

LAIRIG GHRU

GLEN DERRY

6

corrour bothy ■

7

luibeg ■ derry lodge

8

GLEN DEE

river dee

White Bridge

Braemar

Linn of Dee

■ ruigh nah clach

GLEN FESHIE

geldie burn

■ lower geldie

■ bynack lodge

1 Cairn Gorm
2 Loch Avon
3 Loch Etchachan
4 Ben Macdui
5 Derry Cairngorm
6 Cairn Toul
7 Carn a Mhaim
8 Beinn Bhrotain

tarf

▲
N

GLEN TILT

TILT

forest lodge ■

Blair Atholl

Not to scale

I then remembered something I had read in an old Scottish Mountaineering Club Journal: the temperature of the pools remains at two degrees centigrade all year round, however hot the summer. "My God, Scroggie," he gasped, buffing himself to get back some life in his arms, "remind me never to do that again !"

The Lairig Ghru is the premier pass in the British Isles. The Corrieyairack, the Lairig an Lui, the Feshie, the Tilt, the Monega, the Capel Mounth and Jock's Road all have much to recommend them. But in sheer length and ruggedness, in the character of its bothies, in its boulderfields, and in the fact that it cuts between two of the largest lumps of land in these islands, Braeriach and Ben Macdhui, there is nothing to beat *The Lairig*. People know you mean the Lairig Ghru when you say that. The only question left is what the Gael of old meant by the adjective "Ghru". There is a picture of the pass in the old S.M.C. guide to the Cairngorms, one of these pictures that folds out. No other picture of these gloomy, eerie and massive hills has ever stirred my imagination more.

It shows the Lairig Grumach, the word Grumach means gloomy. It seems even more terrifying when compressed into the contraction of a monosyllable "Ghru". Tempting as it is to accept this etymology, let us fold back this sombre picture and think of the Lairig as I observed it again, years after that blazing day when Bob had his dook in the Pools of Dee. Again it was glorious weather and, on that occasion early in the month of June, my friend Dennis and I were crossing the Lairig in a canny drifting from bothy to bothy. So we found ourselves in the evening traversing a vast field of sugar snow which buried most of the boulders. The westering sun struck brightly on the snow and emphasised the natural colour of the rock.

Dennis sat down, and as we smoked a fag he observed a redness in the boulders which protruded from the snow, and various tints of this same colour in the scraggy slopes which rise abruptly on either hand. A ptarmigan's eerie croak echoed in the silence. Dennis has a little Gaelic as I have, but we can make that little go a long way. What we saw was not a gloomy pass. What we saw was a red pass, and the Gaels were nothing in their naming of places, if not simple describers of the scene. "Sydney," said Dennis, with all the complacency and certitude of genius, "It's the Lairig Ruadh."

The geographical termini of this ancient route through the Cairngorms are of course Aviemore and Braemar, and I mention them in that order because it was from west to east in olden times, as Seton Gordon reminds us, that a traffic in eggs was carried on between a Speyside teeming with fecund hens and a good market under Morrone and Creag Choinnich on the banks of Dee.

Between these termini are some twenty nine miles of hill terrain, much of it as high and remote as anything you will get in these islands, and between the piping oyster catchers of such places as Corriemoulzie, Inverey and Claybokie, and those of Lairig Cottage and Coylumbridge there are the chaffinches of Derry Lodge and Luibeg, where the breeze rustles the old Scots pines; the meadow pipits of Carn a' Mhaim; the sandpipers of Corrour; the ptarmigan of the Pools of Dee; and in the Forest of Rothiemurchus, where the heather is high, such rare species as crossbill and crested tit.

In addition, if you are lucky, you may hear the deep croak of raven off Sron na

Lairig or the mewing of buzzard around the Lurcher's Crag; or maybe a golden eagle will drift across your line of vision from the boulders of Coire Bhrochain to the upper recesses of the Tailor's Burn. With the Sron Riach rising before you and Corrie Sputan Dearg, you ford the Lui if it is not in spate, otherwise you have to go further upstream to the new metal bridge. Sometimes in boulders, sometimes in bog and sometimes on bare granite bedrock you breast the brae of lower Carn a' Mhaim, to find yourself gazing at length into the hag-scarred gulf of Glen Geusachan and at Beinn Bhrotain, which bulks dark and big beside it.

Further round, as you drop down into upper Glen Dee, is the Devil's Point, on which there are no more formidable slabs in Scotland, Cairn Toul with its screes, the Soldier's Corrie, and that other evidence of the handiwork of ancient ice, Coire Odhar, from which the bothy below it takes its name; and even now you catch a glimpse of the shining aluminium roof of Corrour. After much hopping over boulders and dragging your feet out of bogs you come to the rushing waters of the Tailor's Burn, where there is gold for those with the patience to pan it, and maybe sit down to eat your piece under that same big rock where the ambitious but ill-fated men of needle and thread died in a Hogmanay blizzard all those years ago.

Next you come to the Allt Choire Mhoir, whose noise you have heard for some time, high up in front of you on the right; ford it, and with the young Dee tearing along below you on the left, start the ascent to the Lairig Ghru proper. Across the glen, and with its inner crags rising to the 4,000 foot plateau, is the mighty amphitheatre of the Garbh Choire where snow lies all year round, and there is a little howff nowadays used by the tigers of the rock and ice climbing fraternity.

Big and broad and littered with boulders, Braeriach rises beside it, forming the left portal of the Lairig, and Coire Bhrochain is gouged out of it so that the hill has a smashed, decayed appearance, infinitely sad and lonely. Beyond the Pools of Dee and the summit boulderfield, and with the thunder of the March Burn behind you, it is a case of gazing down through the cleft of the pass at the lowlands of Spey far away, perhaps golden with evening sun, and behind them, the rolling Monadh Liaths shutting out the west and north. Here there is silence, as if to commemorate a desultory human penetration going back to the dawn of time; a silence broken only by the croak of ptarmigan and emphasized by the granite power of boulder and enclosing crag.

So you begin to drop down the stony track, the boulderfield receding behind you, and the infant Allt Druie picks up strength to the right of you, and beyond it, gleaming with wetness, the dark massiveness of the Lurcher's Crag. You pass the Sinclair hut on your left, where it stands grim and square on a heathery moraine, then jumping the burn follow the long dog-leg of the track through stones, water, peat-bog and red grit till you are below Castle Hill and the first pines of Rothiemurchus begin to shadow the track; protruding roots are slippery under your boots, and fronds brush your shoulder as you trudge along. The iron bridge is ahead, with its embossed information regarding distances and times, and, where I am concerned, beyond Achnagoichan where the Nature Conservancy man lives, the raison d'etre of many a trip through the Lairig over the years, a night with Jock and Margaret McKenzie who farm Upper Tullochgrue.

On the Cairngorm Plateau. Shelter Stone Crag in the middle distance

In 1942, stationed with the Army in camps at Alvie and Pityoulish, I made evening trips to the Lairig and on to the hills round about it. A war department pushbike with back-pedalling brakes would get me to the Piccadilly junction of paths where there is a cairn and a finger-post. One track turns left for Glen More and Loch Morlich; the other climbs between banks of overhanging heather to the last scattered pines of Rothiemurchus, the crossing of the Allt Druie, and the cleft of the Lairig, Braeriach very big and upstanding on the right.

On one occasion I stood on the plateau near this summit, grit, moss, boulders and the big cairn at 4,248 feet, and gazed down into the depths of the Garbh Choire, the massif of Ben Macdhui rising on the far side of Glen Dee. It was perfectly still; only a golden plover cried sadly: and the sky was feathered all over with wisps of high cirrus cloud evenly distributed from horizon to horizon. The sun had set, and these cirrus clouds now caught the last of its light, the wide sky becoming arched with glowing filaments of red fire, and shortly a flush suffused the whole landscape so that I was alone in that barren tundra in a vast holocaust, as it were, of inoffensive flame.

On another occasion, this time with pack, food and sleeping-bag, I struck up the rotten, red rock to the left of the summit of the Lairig, reached the plateau between Creag an Leth-Choin and Ben Macdhui, found the waters of the upper Garbh Uisge where they slide over bedrock or tumble among stones, and followed these down the steep rock-terraces to Loch A'an for a solitary night at the Shelter Stone. Fat cumulus clouds turned gold in the evening light, Cairn Gorm was big, silent and still, and the water of the loch was like a glass reflecting the tors on Bynack More. Again I found myself between Creag an Leth-Choin and Macdhui, the chasm of the Lairig behind me, and this time, after a week of rain, the cloud was rising, so that I followed the ascending base of it, grey and lowering, up the flat, granite boulders which litter the shoulder of Macdhui on this side.

There had been no sunshine in Speyside that day, only teeming rain, but now a shaft of golden sun shot through the cloud, to strike a snowfield which covered the boulders ahead. Its privacy disturbed, an eagle took off, and at the same time the whole canopy of cloud lifted, disclosing the summit of Macdhui, to hang a grey and dour umbrella over the clear tops of the Cairngorms. The shaft of sun disappeared, and I broke into a run, leaping from boulder to boulder, to get to the big summit cairn before it should be lost again in descending thickness and drizzle. The usual rusty bully beef tins were there, friendly in a squalid kind of way, and I gazed round at a scene which I dare say few people, if any, have ever witnessed from Macdhui.

The Cairngorms lay beneath what was now a local bonnet of cloud. Everything else was in sunshine and dazzling with colours, cobalts and browns and bright greens, all the peaks around glowing with the pristine pigments of an illuminated manuscript, as far as distant Lochnagar and Beinn a' Ghlo. Then even the interior gloom began to change, and a violet light stole over the nearby scene, so that my hands reflected it and my clothes, and behind me the Lurcher's Crag turned as mauve as the most voluptuous ling heather. This was not so with Angel Peak, Cairn Toul and the Devil's Point, which rose on the other side of Glen Dee, for these turned an emerald green, so that they stood there like vast jewels, soft and glowing, against that brilliant distant palette of incredible colour.

It lasted only a minute or two, long enough for a ptarmigan to croak, a golden plover to whistle and a discarded fag pack to stir in the breeze; then down came the cloud again and shut everything out. One moment I was in the treasure house of Creosus; the next in a dank, gloomy dungeon; and I turned and made off down the hill as fast as the fitness of twenty two could carry me. However, the display was not over yet: the Lairig still had something to offer although the spectacle had been switched off on Macdhui. For as I dropped down from the bouldery pass, running and leaping out of sheer joie de vivre, a second shaft of sunshine, now low from the north-west, struck through the cloud, this time glancing on the Lurcher's Crag, which rose beetling above me on my right, dark, dreich and dripping. In an instant it was all chocolate brown, shot with gold, and all its algaes and vegetation, invisible heretofore, turned a most brilliant jungle green. This in its turn faded, and I was over the Allt Druie and skelping along through the stones and bogs towards the upper timber of Rothiemurchus when the final act in this drama of colour unfolded itself; the last act before gloaming, twilight, and a Speyside sky studded with stars.

Like a big, red ball the sun suddenly appeared at the very rim of the world, just visible in the narrow aperture between cloud and horizon, and in its rays the mist which now blanketed the whole massif of the Cairngorms began to flush, the greyness turning to a sombre red, so that the hills now seemed mantled in a great hodden-grey plaid stained through and through with the blood of some gigantic wearer. The sun set, the redness returned to common grey, and from the east cool evening stole over a silent world.

CHAPTER TWO

Etchachan Hut.

As I first experienced it in 1938, Corrour bothy was in a beautifully dilapidated condition, just the thing to give a place character. Howffs like the Sinclair hut and the Etchachan hut, hard, bleak and neutral, which were to come along some two decades later, are about as lovable as a frigid wife.

Who were the chaps that were with me during that dull, dry summer week, where across the peat-hags I heard the murmur of the Dee for the first time, howked out bog-stumps from Glen Geusachan for the fire, and watched the evening mist come down, veiling the screes of Carn a'Mhaim in drab grey ?

John Ferguson, sixteen years of age,yet never a boy, was my companion, and we had cycled up from Dundee in a thunderstorm, St. Elmo's fire flickering blue on our handlebars, shared with midges a soaking camping place at Inverey, dumped our bikes at Derry Lodge, and trudged to a bog-girt Dee which in those days had to be forded or not crossed at all.

Loden hat with superimposed pyjama cord and feather, baggy Lovat flannels, voluminous, stiff, anorak in a menacing green colour, and a pair of Laurie's boots with number seven tricounis in them. John smoked his Four Square Red with the air of a man who knows what he is about. In fact it was his ambition on this trip to get up the Black Pinnacle in Coire Bhrochain, to which end our rucksacks were coiled about with hemp line as we clumped across the old wooden footbridge over the Lui, and as we dropped down the bouldery track into Glen Dee, clinked with ostentatiously displayed karabiners and pitons, the latter made to my astute friend's design by a blacksmith friend of his.

If we did not get up the Black Pinnacle, which seemed to haunt the imagination of Hawkhill Place at this time, then it would not be due to any want of resolution on the part of John to lead or me to follow him, and certainly not to any deficiency in the equipment requisite to the task. As to rock-climbing techniques, John was well up in the latest developments of the Munich school, and had the Eiger reared its savage face behind Corrour bothy, John would as readily have tackled it as a piddling protuberance on the crags of Coire Bhrochain.

In the bothy we were joined by one Kenny Strathearn. When the throaty " go-back go-back" utterance of flushed grouse warned us someone was coming, and we saw a tall, bony figure in a brown tweed suit jumping the stepping-stones in the Dee with a suitcase in his hand, we thought we were going to have a regular tenderfoot on our hands. Here was someone, surely, unaccustomed to leaky tents in Corrie Fee or rigorous nights at Sandy Hillocks and Broad Cairn or to the claustrophobic confines of the Glen Doll Hut; but one better adapted to bed-and-breakfast on a good bus route.

We were mistaken. The serene, ironic, grey eyes of this Dundee divinity student had gazed on the like of Corrour bothy before; those gangly shanks had traversed many dour miles of heather, bog and boulder; and those pale, slender fingers, as it turned out, were trained by long experience to the niceties of making oatcakes on smouldering bog-timber, of improvising candles from twine and whatever stalactites of old wax hung stiffly from the shelves and ledges of Corrour.

Together with John and me, this kindly, humorous and philosophic Scot sat by the fire, with the candle flickering, enjoying the romance of being in this decayed bothy which once housed a summer deer forest watcher. The three of us, John, Kenny and myself were lounging in this chiaroscuro of candle and firelight when we were joined by a lone walker, a medical student from Aberdeen by the name of Andrew Brockie as we quickly found out.

In this light, far more revealing than garish electrics or hissing Tilly lamp, we surveyed the torn-up floor with joists and bent nails exposed, moist walls of quarried granite with the protective panelling gone, the underside of a tarry felt roof, the waterproof qualities of which were merely retrospective, and at the far end of the bothy from the fireplace, a ladder propped up against a sagging loft where lay the ancient mattress reputedly infested with fleas.

There were one or two chairs, barely any longer in a condition to stand the weight of the deerstalker of old, but rickety and tied up with string; a table, dark with paraffin stains and scabby with wax, which seemed to lean up against the wall with the last of its strength; and in the corner to the right of the fireplace, a dirty old press with its door off its hinges, crammed with mildewed paper bags of oatmeal, half-empty packets of tea screwed up at the top, dusty bottles of paraffin and meths, tins of salt gone solid with damp, a can or two of Fray Bentos or Ambrosia rice presented to the bothy by anonymous donors, and a half-used condensed milk tin with matches twisted round with paper to wedge up the holes: crammed that is to say, with the decaying evidence of desultory habitation over the years.

Andrew Brockie, a humorous chap with dark, wavy hair, peered out of his sleeping bag, his head supported by rucksack and folded breeks, and a fag in his mouth. In the instant intimacy of bothy life, he had already risen high in our estimation, both by the likeable quality of his character and by the fact, as he complaisantly informed us, that he had fallen a hundred feet practising rock-climbing in Rubislaw quarry, Aberdeen and got away with it.

He saw socks steaming on strings, wet, muddy boots stuffed with newspaper, a dim jumble of rucksacks and gear, and in the ashes around the hearth an indescribable guddle of greasy tin plates, primus stoves, chipped enamelled mugs, and bashed billy-cans with sodden tea-leaves at the bottom of them. He saw also, as we did, the glow of the bog-stump fire, with all that shifting phantasmagoria of figures and shapes which the imagination conjures up in the flaming life of that element, which is at the very heart of domesticity, as it is of life itself.

Outside, the great hills were silent in the darkness and mist, the Dee followed its age-long impetuosities between Braeriach and Torry, and in all the great head of Glen Dee, bogs, stones and heather clumps, there was not so much as the squawk of a grouse, the scream of vixen, or surreptitious movement of stag. The faces of John and Kenny, the one pondering and intent, the other bland and serene, were half in light, half in shadow; a log settled in the fire, and Brockie took a sip at his tea. "This," he said, and he expressed the thoughts of us all, "is what I call home."

John and I got up the Black Pinnacle all right, not by any means by the direct route, which was way beyond our capabilities at this time, but working our way along a connecting ridge from the face of Coire Bhrochain, so that at last we sat at the top, looking behind at the piled pancakes of granite which rise to the summit plateau, or down the immense drop in front of us to the shattered screes of the corrie floor. Beyond the corrie the land fell away to the head of Glen Dee, brown heather, patches of yellow sphagnum moss, and greenery of various hues interspersed with grey boulders; and at the far side of this rose massive slopes, dark and stony and deeply cleft by the gullies of the Allt Choire Mhoir and Tailor's Burn, to the upper parts of Macdhui. The sky was pearly grey, a breeze stirred in the buttresses and gullies around us, and we heard the brittle croak of a ptarmigan far, far away.

John, as I said, had regular climbing-boots on with number seven tricounis, their small iron teeth already much worn with jaunts in the Doll and Corrie Fee, as also in the Cuillin of Skye from which he had recently returned, not only filled with a zest for Window Buttress and the Cioch West, but also well versed in bawdy climbing-songs learned from an English climbing party in Glen Brittle.

His fingers as he now built a little cairn of stones on top of the pinnacle, had a kind of capable clumsiness, the hair that escaped below that Loden hat was thick, brown and wavy, and it was difficult to think of that gaunt, grave face which bent earnestly over the work, as belonging to a boy of sixteen. There was a pixie, however, in this intent student of buttress and wall, which continually asserted the claims of the fantastic in a nature which oscillated incongruously between the facetious and the profound. Finishing his cairn, and wedging an empty date packet in it with our names pencilled on, he looked at me with his merriest and wickedest grin. "Get out the barbed wire, Sydney," he said "and we'll abseil down to Corrour."

The Wells of Dee, the ultimate source of the highest river in Britain lie over the back of the Braeriach from the Coire Bhrochain side, and John and I explored around until we found them, our boots scrunching on the grits and gravels of that bleak sub-Arctic plateau. As if eager to have a look at the outside world, or alternatively anxious to escape as quickly as possible from Pluto's kingdom below, this first cold freshet of the Dee snotters so briskly out of holes among boulders as to raise a question where the head of water can be which is high enough above the altitude of these wells to make this water burst forth so vigorously here at around 4000 feet.

It cannot be anywhere else in Scotland, for there is no higher land, and on whatever dubious geological grounds, it has been suggested to me that the head of water is in the Hartz Mountains, from where, assisted by an impermeable layer of rock under the North Sea, sufficient water-pressure survives to account for these lonely Wells of Dee. Like the belief that there are plesiosaurs in Loch Ness, I hope this theory never comes to be disproved, for it has been a staple of my bothy-conversation for years, and I would not know what to do without it. So John and I, not without mock ritual, drank from the Wells of Dee, then dropped down to the boulders of the Lairig, and so back to Corrour bothy, where we were now the sole

The Black Pinnacle of Coire Bhrochain

inhabitants, the tall, gangling figure of Kenny Strathearn and the stocky Andrew Brockie, swarthy and athletic, having moved on.

John and I had had the company of Kenny the day before, when we went up Macdhui by the Tailor's Burn, with due caution descending Castle Gates Gully to visit the Shelter Stone, then returned to Corrour by lonely Loch Etchachan under its crags, and a second crossing of Macdhui summit with its outlook to nearby Cairn Toul and the Devil's Point, looming menacingly over the plateau edge, and to a monarchic Nevis seventy miles away.

Kenny, a student not only of Patristic literature but also of everything in the hills, showed us where to look for Cairngorm crystals, and we found a few broken fragments of smoky colour with a flat, polished facet or two showing. Previous to the arrival of this amiable polymath at Corrour, John and I scrambled up the bare, granite ridge which rises beside the Soldier's Corrie to the summit boulderfield of Cairn Toul, moved across to the Devil's Point, where Beinn Bhrotain bulks up beyond Glen Geusachan and Sgor an Dubh dominates the Glen Einich side, then with the black crags rising higher and higher on our right, dropped down to the bothy, disturbing a parcel of stags in the steep grazings of Coire Odhar.

Silence was the keynote of these first essays of ours in the purlieus of the Lairig Ghru, silence and grey skies and only the mournful cry of golden plover, the croak of ptarmigan and chuckle of deep-burrowed waters to emphasize an otherwise nothingness of sound so profound and universal over heather, bog and boulder that you could hear the hissing in your ears. There was also an eeriness, especially at night, so that when I shut the creaky door of the bothy behind me and took the billy-can to the burn for water, I felt an unseen presence in the darkness, not perhaps terrifying but vaguely menacing, so that I hastened back to the fire with beating heart and the short hairs stirring on the back of my neck. The demonic and the supernatural are easier to believe in mist and the blackness of a night at the head of Glen Dee with the uneasy stir of heather in the wind.

My friend Les Bowman had implied this in a postcard to me some little time before, date-stamped Aviemore. This lean, dark man had just walked the Lairig for the first time. He wrote in his neat, somewhat feminine hand, "You shut off the stove in Corrour, and the silence rushes in at you under the door."

It was twenty years on from these early days that the events of Chapter One took place, with Bob McLean diving into the biggest of the Pools of Dee and finding the heat becoming an enemy, not a friend. Bob's nose was already a bit burnt by the sun, that rather handsome nose of his which Norma Merrilees in the years to come was laughingly to say she married him for, and had not yet sniffed the insanitary miasma of the Nile; as those grey eyes had yet to look upon the scrubby Aussie outback, crowded Bangkok, Kanchenjunga in the rosy light of dawn, and the sun-baked cuds of the Khyber Pass.

Now I directed them to the view which opened to our right. Even I had put on my shirt against the sun, though it was only four o'clock and in May month. "Look over there, Bob," I said. "That decayed-looking cavity on Braeriach is Coire Bhrochain, and you should see the Black Pinnacle stuck on the crags at the back. " The fact that Coire Bhrochain means "Porridge Pot" did not seem relevant to my

18

Corrour Bothy.

purpose, so I kept this information to myself. "That's the thing John Ferguson and I were on top of in 1938." Amiably sarcastic, Bob took the opportunity of alluding to the vast discrepancy between our ages; and then, "Sorry Scroggie," he said; "but there's no sign of this Black Pinnacle of yours up there."

Was he looking at the right hill, I said menacingly; and there followed one of those mock altercations and cheerful slanging matches with which it has always been customary for Bob and me to vary the strict business of getting from one place to another in the hills. "You're havering, Scroggie," my bearded friend concluded, at the same time however, offering me a conciliatory fag: "There's no pinnacle up there now, and in my opinion there never was. It was just something invented by you and your pal Ferguson in conjunction with the Scottish Mountaineering Club, with a view to the enhancement of the hill, what's its name, Braeriach. The only time you were ever on it was when you were asleep and dreaming."

By this time we were moving along towards the Allt Choire Mhoir. The Dee rushed past us on our right, boulders were hot to the touch, and the stretches of peat-bog, normally so sucky and glutinous, were cracked like the Gobi desert. "McLean," I said, my hand on the back of his rucksack and my big willow thumb-stick probing the route; "it looks as if there are two blind men on this trip."

Dr. Taylor had not yet constructed his clattery metal bridge over the Dee at Corrour, so we plowtered through the water, thumped across the brown, baked peat-hags, and went into the bothy for a sit in the shade. It is summer indeed when you have to get out of the sun, and Bob and I were glad to get our backs against the cool, stone wall, stretch our legs on the dirt, and in the coolness and dimness of the interior get out a packet of dates. "They are tramped flat by bare feet," said Bob, handing me a sticky fibrous lump: "But they are the cheapest and most nutritious food you can get."

"I knew a fellow once, Bob," I was saying, when a stranger came into the bothy. I paused to say hullo on behalf of the two of us, then continued: "It was in August, 1930, the night of the biggest thunderstorm there's ever been in these islands, and this fellow spent it alone in a tent at the Pools of Dee. The storm covered the whole country and went on all night. Thousands of cattle - beasts got killed, pigs, sheep, goats and hens: the sky was lit up continuously, and observatories were counting a hundred flashes of lightning a minute. There was not a drop of rain, and through it all Jimmy Ritchie lay cowering in his tent in the Lairig. He said it was the worst experience he ever had."

Our visitor listened politely to this recital, which was partly designed to impress him with my knowledge of these parts, then gazing at my tin leg and at the same time, jalousing that I was blind, he said in a quiet, sincere kind of voice, "Does nothing ever daunt you ?"

I thought of all the things that daunt me, and they are many, but replied that my friends were a pretty dauntless breed, and once we were in places like the Lairig there was nothing for it, since I could not escape, but just tag along quietly.

McLean and I rather got the impression, talking about him later, that our visitor might have been a student minister, but at any rate we listened now as he told us about his adventures on the high plateau that burning day. "I took off all my clothes," he said, "and wandered around a bit in the sun. Then I thought I'd look for some shade, and since the only shade was beside the big summit cairn of Braeriach I went across there. But I couldn't get into it. The shade was already occupied by every creeping, hopping, buzzing thing between Glen Einich and the Lairig Ghru. For Homo Sapiens there was no comfortable shelter."

There is only one thing worse than a blizzard for tiring you out on the hill, and that is a long day in the sun. We were getting niggly as we hunched along wearily, a bit morose on the last stony miles to Luibeg, sniffing the odour of hot resin from the pines.

"You and your bridge, Scroggie," growled McLean. He was alluding to the fact that I had said it would be a good idea to cross the Lui by the fancy, new metal bridge, rather than ford in the old place further down. "You've put a good two miles on to the journey."

I was still meditating some vitriolic retort as we turned across to the bothy, and the smell of woodsmoke, whence came a cheery hail in the Aberdeen tongue from that most affable of deer stalkers, the burly Bob Scott. "I doot ther's nae room in the bothy; it's ower full wi' they Etchachan loons, I'll let ye into the stable."

McLean and I dismissed that idea, saying we would sleep on a green haugh by the burn. At 1350 feet it would be airy enough to put paid to the midges.

Four years previous to this trip with McLean, and ten years after my getting blown-up in the war, I had my first visit to the hills as a blind man with a tin leg, with good friend Les Bowman as my eyes.

"Young Scrog," he said, making play as he often did of the slight disparity in our ages;

"Let's do a trip to Corrour." I could imagine his face, the big green eyes, the high cheek bones, the fastidious lips, sallow complexion, head of thick, dark, wavy hair, greying, as I had seen him in the tumultuous precincts of Santa Maria dei' in Florence all these years ago.

The idea was staggering, of my setting out and returning as a disabled person to the locality which more than any other for me is symbolic of the hills. In the very thought of it I heard the babbling of the Lui and the Dee, the breeze in the pines, the calls of tits and chaffinches; saw the red scar of the Lairig Ghru track, and through the haughs and the heather Sròn Riach of Ben Macdhui. I could hear the sooking of boots in the peat-hags under Devil's Point and the creak of the old bothy door as we went into Corrour. More to the point I heard him say, "Well, what about it?" "You bet," I replied.

CHAPTER THREE

There is nothing like a good talisman when you are in the hills, and it does not have to be anything very exotic or very expensive, a scarab from Tutenkhamen's tomb, the green eye of the little yellow god, or anything like that. Anything will do, an old hat with pyjama cord round it, a greasy, insanitary anorak which has been with you since the beginning of your adventures in heather, bog and boulder; anything that gives you the feeling that having it will have the effect of warding off the evil chance and enabling you safely to attain your objective and get back again.

Anything with a spice of danger in it, coal-mining, deep-sea trawling, soldiering and the like, wandering around the hills makes you superstitious, so that some kind of talisman in the interests of self preservation you come to regard being as necessary as rations, sleeping-bag and primus stove; and in fact the latter in my case, since it had been in my possession for thirty four years, is pretty well in the talisman class itself. Any trip without it, I feel in my bones, could be the trip from which I might never come back.

As religion is an actual safeguard against psychic danger, so superstition is an imagined safeguard against physical danger; and so it was, on the last day of April, 1955, that when I set out with Les for my first blind trip into the hills I carried with me by way of talisman a rusty old karabiner which, because of its ancient associations with Eagle Ridge, Lochnagar, and Gardyloo Buttress of Ben Nevis, for me it had all the properties required in a really reliable talisman.

I fastened the spring clip to my rucksack frame, the very rucksack I was wearing when I got blown up in Italy ten years before, and set out from Derry Lodge with Les's hand under my oxter, fully convinced that with this karabiner attached there was no doubt but that the expedition to Corrour bothy would be a success. I do not know that Bob Scott entirely shared this optimism of mine, but at any rate he said goodbye to us in the neighbourhood of Derry Lodge.

Although Bob was just a voice to me, his loud, cheery delivery in the Aberdeen tongue had massive reserves of certainty and determination in it. This stalker who had recently taken up residence in the remotest house in the Cairngorms inspired the belief that he would be a good friend, but the absolute reverse to climbers and hillwalkers who did not play the game.

I seemed to see this brawny, purposeful figure weighing me up, shaking his head dubiously over the prospect of a blind man, perhaps for the first time in history, disappearing from view over the shoulder of Cairn a'Mhaim. Bob's fears were to be allayed as the years went by and he got accustomed to seeing me around Luibeg in the company of one pal or another, trudging away up the Derry to the Shelter Stone, or following the same route which I now essayed for the first time with Les.

But now I could imagine him muttering to himself as he saw that black parka disappearing amongst the pines, that funny-looking Yankee rucksack, that big stick and the limping tin leg gait. "Gosh," I could hear him saying, "There's been wooden legs here afore, but never but never a blind bugger awa' to Corrour that I mind o'."

Bob Scott — sadly missed by the regulars at his bothy

My rusty talisman, redolent of days spent on mica'd granite in the days gone by, seems to have been effective in its principle task, that of getting Les and me to the bothy that afternoon, though I think these half-dozen miles were the longest and roughest in their effect on my body and soul that I ever traversed anywhere. Yet the joy and exhilaration I experienced as Les and I eventually stood near the bank of the Dee, the sense of sheer triumph, would have compensated for much more in the way of aching muscles, chafed stump, and the feeling that dogged me from time to time, as it did Les too, that perhaps we might not manage it after all. But the timber of Derry Lodge lay far behind us now, the meadow pipits and wheatears of Carn a'Mhaim, the bouldery descent into Glen Dee, and best of all, what the blurred vision of Les had taken to be a lingering snow-patch at the foot of the Devil's Point, turned out to be a brand-new aluminium roof which somebody had put on Corrour.

The bothy now lay at no great distance over the peat-hags, but the Dee intervened, swirling in spate, and here in the immediate foreground was another novelty which the ingenuity of man had introduced to the locality in the seventeen years since I had last stood on this spot, heard those same waters running, and felt on my cheek that same breeze from the stony recesses of the Lairig Ghru. In the old days you had to ford the river, and in my mind's eye I could see lanky Kenny Strathearn, killed at the Rhine crossing a decade ago, cautiously negotiating the stepping-stones in just such a spate as this. Now however, as Les informed me, there was a telegraph pole driven into each bank of the river, and it would be a matter of no great difficulty, though it would be interesting, to cross the river by means of the two parallel wires slung between them.

"You go first," said Les, getting me into position for the start; "and I'll just have a fag and watch you fall in." I had no notion to get a wetting, let alone fracture my skull on a boulder, and this is where my karabiner showed it had a practical application in the expedition as well as its now proven function as talisman. I had a bit of rope tied round my waist, and when I had got on to the bottom wire I clipped this bit of rope with me inside it to the top wire by means of the karabiner, leant back nonchalantly over the swirling water, supported by this sliding belay, and stretched my arms out wide. The eternal child still lurks in the rugged adult bosom. "Les," I yelled against the noise of the spate; "look, no hands."

Nostalgia for a Lairig, and such as "*The Lairig*", which I never expected to trudge again, found some kind of expression in verses written by me long after the experience that touched them off, long before that unimaginable day when Les and I shuffled across the wire bridge, threaded our way through the peat bog on the other side, and lifted the latch of Corrour, a Corrour perhaps altered in externals but still preserving, as it will preserve for ever, its place as a key symbol in that complex psychological state which we vaguely call "the hills".

> "Little the map bears witness to the
>   ground
> When beauty is the question first in
>   mind,
> Nor is the truth of Ben Macdhui
>   found
> In surveys of the hill of any
>   kind,
> Saving some contoured cart that's first and
>   last
> Etched in the biting joy of mountain
>   days
> And printed in remembrance of the
>   past.
> Where is the golden crucible whose
>   blaze
> Transmutes the melting summits
>   one by one,
> And mixes western magic in a
>   sky
> Lovely with flame above
>   Leviathan,
> That's red with rich drops from that
>   alchemy.

Thy elixir, O, Lord, we seek
    in vain
To turn life's image back to life
    again."

By the time I trod the Lairig with McLean in 1959, our shadow sliding across the boulders of the Pools of Dee and heat pulsating on us, I already had a lot of blind hills behind me, and so the verses that came out of this trip reflect a different mood, one in which my return to the wilds of Braeriach is a fait accompli rather than an idee fixe. "If you're not careful, Scroggie ....." McLean was being ironic rather than prophetic, ".... you'll be getting into the anthologies one of these days."

"Is this the Lairig then, this halcyon
    way;
Thick terror should by rights possess the
    soul,
Madness by night, uneasy haste by day,
To slip the skinny clutch of loitering
    troll.
Where is the storm that shrieks, the
    silent snow
Drifting that ruck of melancholy bone
There where the Grey Man's monstrous
    footfalls go
And reeling warlocks ring the Tailor's
    Stone.
This is the impish genii the sun,
And his the hand and his the shimmering
    brain
And his the laughter when the wheel was
    spun.
This is some other age, some other land,
And we by noonday's mirage pilgrims twain
Upon the golden road to Samarakand."

When Les and I got to Derry Lodge that April day in 1955, and before we had got our rucksacks on or fallen in with tweed-clad Bob Scott, we sat in the stale fag-smoke of the old Standard, eating bacon-and-egg pie and gazing with gloomy foreboding through steamy windows at a downpour of rain which had just come on, and which thrashed the pines and stotted off the chucky-stones of the road with a vehemence that seemed determined to deflect us from our intention. Les was especially lugubrious, but in a way that suggested he would not have his ambitions flouted by weather, however bad, and would if necessary resort to masochism if that was the only means left of pleasure between a wet Derry Lodge and a forlorn and teeming Corrour.

April had been a very fine month, and this had been one of the elements, I

Derry Lodge.

suppose, in the germination of the idea of this trip in the unfathomable mind of my friend. Now he stared balefully at a turn in the weather which seemed cynically laid on by the gods to thwart him. "It would have to bloody rain." As if this was not enough there was a peal of thunder so Wagnerian in scale that its reverberations in the surrounding hills seemed as if they would never rumble into silence again. It was immediately preceded by a violet glare which quivered on the streaming windscreen, and followed by an intensification of the rain so that we could not hear each other for the noise of it drumming on the roof.

Thunder is said to clear the air, and sure enough on this occasion the black cloud passed away, the rain went off, and it was in wan sunshine and a cool westerly breeze that Les and I made the trip to Corrour, no more than a wee spitter of a shower now and again, and the Devil's Point gleaming, wet black and clear of cloud to its very summit. This peal of thunder, the only one I have ever heard in the purlieus of the Lairig, makes its appearance in verses written after this trip, but with a connotation quite different from what it conveyed to Les and me as we sat gloomily in the beleaguered Standard.

> "I had not seen Corrour these seventeen
>   years
> Nor trod the track that turns through
>   antique pines,
> The rough, red track where Geusachan
>   appears,
> The Devil's Point, and Bhrotain's dark-
>   etch'd lines.
> And well I saw him then, that other me,
> Him of the stalker's eye, the athlete's
>   leg,
> Wayward in much, in hills pure constancy,
> Myself when young a mile from Luibeg.
> Small wonder that the lightning flashed
>   that day,
> And thunder loud on crag and cornice
>   rolled
> And boomed and snarled and grumbling died
>   away.
> The gods thus spoke, the gods of hill and
>   glen:
> This is our man, we know his face of old,
> He has but slept, behold he comes again.

A touch of evening pinkness now in the clouds over Coire Odhar, Les and I entered the bothy, dumping our sacks for the meantime at the door, to find ourselves in a very different Corrour from the one Les remembered from his solo trip through the Lairig, myself from those days in 1938 when the clink of John Ferguson's pitons reminded a Kenny Strathearn and an Andrew Brockie that the Dundee boys were not just up there to stare at the scenery. Gone were the table and chairs, loft, ladder and press. There was now no flooring at all, not even the mutilated planks and joists you tripped over of old; only beaten, bare peat soil, relieved along the back wall by plucked heather laid down for bedding.

The old tarry felt roof, as we had already observed, had been redone in gleaming sheet aluminium; there was a kind of cooking-bench in rough concrete on the same wall as the door: and the door itself, solid and true, was in striking contrast to the creaky, friendly, old wreck we remembered. Only the fireplace seemed not to have changed, though surely it had a grate in it before; but there was the same granite hearth now under my questing fingers where wet boots had steamed on my previous stay, the same big mantlestones, though lacking their wooden shelf, where candles had guttered in dusty bottles, and socks dried on strings.

Then the bothy had been friendly and hospitable and somehow mysterious in its ruin and dilapidation, pregnant with a sense of impending romance and adventure. You would not have been surprised to hear the door creak open at any time, to admit, blinking in candlelight, a Wolf of Badenoch, a Bonny Prince Charlie, or wild cattle-drover with bare, hairy legs, brogues, and tattered, mud-stained plaid. Now the bothy had a more clinical air, as if the planners had moved in, and though it was obviously wind and weather tight, and would remain so for decades, it had lost much of its character in the process. The body of Corrour had risen from the grave into which it had virtually collapsed during the War, but it had become dissociated from the soul we remembered.

If this is not preserved in the archives of some climbing-club, then it must eke out a fitful existence in the memory of such as myself, so that it will be with us in the end that the old Corrour will go to its rest, the last of that couthy old soul to fizzle out in oblivion. If the door opened now to admit a sanitary inspector, truant officer or occupational psychologist, you would not be surprised. You would only half-open your eye from your sleeping-bag, then close it again. If the Wolf of Badenoch and Bonny Prince Charlie and the cattle-drovers are still around, the latter with their dogs, their hazel cromaks and their Gaelic oaths, then it is the Shelter Stone or nothing for them now; for this new Corrour is clean out of their ambit. Too securely attached to the door to be easily wrenched off by souvenir-hunters - the bothy in general has little left now to offer to vandals - a metal plaque informs the curious who it was that renovated Corrour and when, and this Les now read out to me in the last of the good light.

There was a quietness everywhere except for the distant ripple of the Dee, the breeze stirred only gently, and dark Carn a' Mhaim, scattered with innumerable screes, seemed about to retire for the night. The old granite walls of the bothy were bare and dour and reassuring. "I didn't know it was built then." Les's recital, half interested, half off-hand, informed me that Corrour first took up its place in the Wilderness in 1877. "My Grannie was only a lassie of eighteen; and that's the age I was when I came here first." Les was inclined to be mordant out of habit, even when he was not feeling that way. "Sydney, you've got here again ...." rummaging about in his sack for grub ".... but don't forget you've still to get back."

Looking South through the Lairig Ghru.

One howling winter day in the twenties, the hapless Baird and Barrie had failed to get back to civilization from Corrour, and some psychic miasma from this tragedy, perhaps the first in the Scottish hills relating purely and simply to the pastime of hill-walking, still hangs round the bothy where they spent their last night alive. For it is as much what happened there in the past as the fabric of the place itself which gives a building its flavour and personality. Its history has as potent an effect on sojourners as its topography, and it is hard to lie in Corrour, as Les and I did that night without experiencing a shudder of horror. It could be your fate to perish, as it was that of Baird and Barrie, in the blinding blizzard between Coire Odhar and Glen Einich. There was no more said then on the potential hazard affecting our return to Derry Lodge next day. Certainly, by the feel of the weather there would be no blizzard flurrying between Dee and Lui, and having pushed through the psychological barrier which loomed so ominously at the outset of this trip, what fear had we of anything uneventful happening between here and the seven miles back down the Lairig.

You do not get two people chatting in Corrour bothy without some talk of the spook which is said to haunt the Cairngorms, and lying in our sleeping-bags in that dramatic flickering candlelight I remember so well, we were close enough to his beat to begin talking about the Big Grey Man of Ben Macdhui.

I reminded Les of what might have been, or for that matter might not have been, as we drew on our fags and sipped some Cointreau. I was telling him of my own experience of the Big Grey Man and describing a night alone at the Shelter Stone in 1941.

"The loch glimmered behind his silhouette in the twilight, and I saw him pace slowly out of the blackness at one side of the water into the blackness at the other."

Said Les in a matter of fact voice of comment. "Well, if you didn't see him, Sydney, then nobody ever made out a better case that he did."

Editor's Note on Bob Scott and Corrour bothy
Bob Scott, deer stalker, salmon fisherman and handyman was Mar Estate keeper at Lui Beg Cottage on the Lairig Ghru path from 1947 until 1977, and he revelled in the society of the young climbers who used his bothy and whom he controlled with an iron hand. Sadly, he died of a lingering illness in 1981, and is remembered as one of the great characters of the Cairngorms.

Corrour bothy below Devil's Point, built last century to house a summer deer-watcher, would have collapsed had the Cairngorm Club not taken action to stop the rot. The renovation was carried out by climbers, Cairngorm Club members and friends, and those of the Lairig and Moray Mountaineering Club. Cement and building materials had to be carried to the site.

CHAPTER FOUR

On top of Devil's Point on a June morning

Enjoying ourselves in Corrour bothy, the question now cropped up of why our fascination for this place 1,850 feet up in the wilderness, under the black crag of Devil's Point , laying on a mattress of wiry heather within damp, dour walls. It was easier for us to get to grips with this strange choice than amongst the multitudinous artifacts of a post-Industrial Revolution environment as evinced by our native Dundee, some of them attractive enough, yet to fulfill something deep in the soul, we had to withdraw from them for a wilderness experience and the feeling of being out on a limb.

The soul of Les, mind you, was less taken up with metaphysics than with his fag, his dram, and the cosiness of his tattered old eiderdown quilt sewn up to make a sleeping-bag. He listened with benign indulgence as I held forth on the subject of why it is that people living in Dundee tenements and working in Dundee mills find it necessary, some of them from time to time, to pack bergans, to put on big boots, and head for Shangri-La, Ultima Thule, Nirvana or Tyr nan Og, however they think of it in the depths of their souls, in the shape of the Lairig Ghru or some other such psychological antipodes.

What is it that the town lacks that they have to go to their Lairig to find it, or at any rate, some credible substitute for it; and what is it, on the other hand, the Lairig lacks, that they have to get back to the town again for those things, whatever its inadequacy in other respects, which the town had to offer and the Lairig has not. The souls of people who go to the hills must, it seems, always oscillate with a view to intermittent fulfilment between a flat overlooking St. James' Park, as you might say, and one of the Shiant isles.

In the toils of this same dichotomy, the Bishop of Brechin says that when he comes to retire he cannot think which he would prefer, the heart of megalopolis with the best of what civilization has to offer, or the smell of bog myrtle, the roar of the surge and the piping oyster-catchers of a Hebridean island.

"In Corrour bothy," said Les, breaking in with friendly irony on my rhetorical flight, so far as it had gone, "there are certainly no evidences of high civilization, except in so far as there are some mangled vestiges of it in ourselves, but neither is there the smell of bog myrtle and all that romantic Celtic garbage of yours. There is only the smell of old fry-ups, an insanitary earth floor which Fraser Darling blamed for the high incidence of still-born babies in West Highland crofts, and a big pile of rusty cans outside which have no connection, so far as I can see, with the salvation of our souls."

Years of intimacy, some differences almost reaching to the point of blows, has taught me always to take careful note of what Les says, for truths often hovered in the background of his ironies. Although he pointed his words at flaws in my thesis I knew he was on my side, so I rambled on with other aspects, as I saw them, of the psychology of chaps who go to the hills.

In every direction round the lonely bothy where Les and I now lay chewing the rag, but at a considerable remove from it, lay a world divided and re-divided against itself, power-block against power-block, class against class, race against race, and ideology against ideology: a world where politics were motivated less by noble aspirations than by greed and ambition; where economies were either mismanaged by ignorance and incompetence, or manipulated for dishonest ends; and where a vast majority of people were too badly off, a small minority too richly endowed, for their good.

Beyond the sprawling Cairngorms, and even interpenetrating them here and there, was a world which could be said by optimists to be in a state of revolution; by pessimists, in a state of collapse: but in either case, a world by no means calculated to confer peace upon its inhabitants, either the outer peace of settled, thriving, purposeful life, or the inner peace and sense of oneness with some great united effort that is the mark of well-integrated souls.

Beyond this world - the geophysical receptacle, that is, of its human counterpart - order, stability and silence, together with what inscrutable end informs it all, reached through a wilderness of light-years to the stars; yet not five minutes from Corrour, inherent in burn, peat-hag and bog, the scarred flanks of Braeriach and Macdhui, in the Pools of Dee and in the boulders of the Lairig, that same peace, stability and silence of interstellar space closed us round, Les and me, in defiance of a jarring world.

We were the only discordant note, it seemed to me, in that vast harmony of hill and glen, for in our souls did we not carry a microcosm of all the crimes and follies of mankind. Neither devastated nor embellished by the hand of man, the Lairig, dark and brooding as it now was, stood neutral in the conflicts of goods and evils that distracted the world of man. That neutrality we could not effect.

We could not bend it one way or the other, buy it, threaten it, deceive it, cajole it. We had not got the power, even if we had been arrogant enough, misguided enough or crazy enough to attempt it. Perhaps, on the other hand, it could affect us, this vast enclave of order, integration, stability and beauty with which we were surrounded, touching our minds and souls with such emanations from its nature as might yet be palpable by two corrupted pilgrims from the world outside. If this was so, might not it be a raison d'etre indeed for such a ploy as that of Les and me that day, granted we had some faint susceptibility to what the Lairig had to offer, the capacity to slough off at least some of the skin of a decadent civilization in exchange.

Les was getting sleepy, but he rallied himself and lit another fag. My pipe I had stuck for safety in a boot, and it was too awkward to reach. "Carry on, Sydney," he said; "you've got the ball at your feet."

"Besides," I continued, glad that Les was too sleepy to be argumentative, "down there in Dundee you lived in a world crammed with insoluble problems, political, economic, industrial and sociological. Every B.B.C. news bulletin implied them, every chance word with stranger or friend confirmed them, every institution or society embodied and perpetuated them. There seemed a positive universal will that nothing must be made to work, so that only by grasping this fact could you make sense of the whole messy set-up at all. In addition to this climate of failure which settled on all the navigable and traversible surface of the world, there was the inner life of man, a veritable hotchpotch of problems, some of them caused by the world situation, some of them effecting it, so shifting and complex and subterranean that it was impossible to analyse them for a start, let alone work out their solution.'

"Hope deferred maketh the heart sick, and this is as true of the hope that your problems may be solved, and those of the world too, as it is that you may win a fortune on the pools or some fair lady's hand. What if we should devise a substitute problem now and again, not so easy that it can be simply solved, yet not so hard it does not permit of solution, granting we apply to it the maximum of mind, body and moral fibre of which we are capable; and so kidding ourselves, at least for a time, that in the solving of this problem, the achieving of this end, all the problems that bedevil the world and us are at an end, and the millenium is at hand. What joy would there not be, what exhilaration, what sense of freedom in the enactment and consummation of it, as in the day getting to Corrour.

"Every expedition, in its inception, struggles, successes, by this argument is a triumphant solving for a time of the problems of the world and the baffling conundrums of the soul. Viewed in this light, together with the beauty, peace and stability we spoke about before, each hill-trip, and they are all in their way successful, brings a catharsis to those who have the insight fully to perceive the horrors of the world."

That was quite some mouthful to deliver to a man who was asleep. The candle would burn itself out, and meantime, as I settled down for the night I went over my notions again on the subject of why people go to the hills. It all seemed very complicated, but "Och, well," I thought to myself as I pulled the woolly hat over my eyes, "The hills are beautiful anyway, and maybe that's reason enough."

I lay pondering about the hills being beautiful, and the tens and thousands of tourists who come every year to gaze at the heather in bloom, the lochs shimmering in the sun, and the birch trees trembling in the breeze from Tyr nan Og; come for an aesthetic counterblast to the ugliness or standardization of a Glasgow, Manchester or Atlanta, Georgia, or wherever human urban blasphemy has risen against the natural order of things. And they carry back with them in their souls, as well as in colour film, some smattering of the cosmic order, the beauty that exists in such superfluity in the hills.

Yet this does not elucidate the rationale of the chap who puts his rucksack on his back and trudges away into Rothiemurchus Forest, his objective distant Corrour bothy or Luibeg, requiring endurance for the boulders of the Pools of Dee, the wind from the summits, and spartan howff or bothy for accommodation: in response to the questioning, the desire for fulfilment, the vague feeling of pilgrimage to a holy place whatever the unconscious urge may be that willy-nilly directs the traveller there.

There is indeed beauty enough on the fringes of the wilderness without the necessity of effort to reach its heart. The seeker of the lonely places is looking for something deeper. And if this is true of one with eyes to see and two sound legs for walking, then how much more must it be true of myself, discovering as I did with Les, that the experience was not one whit less valid, totally blind than when I could see. I would ponder this mystery, but for the present my rucksack under my head and my wooden leg with its muddy boot beside me, I would follow my friend's example and go to sleep. I could not hear Les breathing, roof and stone walls were still, and the silence which is manufactured in such superabundance up there in the Lairig slipped almost audibly under the door.

Since the publication of Affleck Gray's book on the Big Grey Man of Ben Macdhui, an event which caused astonishment in 1972, there is no need any longer for us to rely, for our knowledge of this supernatural phenomenon, on snippets of information picked up from fellow-howffers under the Shelter Stone, or from chance acquaintances in Luibeg, Ryvoan, Findouran Lodge, Corrour and the Sinclair Hut.

The "Greyman", in Gaelic the Fear Liath Mhor, is better known now than ever he was before, and it is perhaps this glare of publicity coupled with a natural surreptitiousness in his character which has caused him to be less in evidence in recent years, despite the flood of potential observers now discharged into the Cairngorms under the banner of Glen More Lodge climbing school and a thousand other organisations who look upon the hills less as a poetical and metaphysical experience than as an area for toughening up the young, reforming the delinquent, or re-integrating the psyche of the mentally defective. He has retired to the recesses of the Lairig, this sixteen foot spectre, and except as a topic of conversation has made no appearances on Ben Macdhui this many a decade so far as I know.

Rats are said to desert a sinking ship, and it is possible that some premonition of

Shelter Stone, Ben Macdhui — home for climbers and mice

disaster has stirred in the mind of the Big Grey Man, some penetration of the hills, for example, on the part of horrid Western Civilization, and that this has had the effect of making him slip away to some part of the globe as yet beyond the avaricious intentions of industrial man.

It was four years after that night with Les Bowman that I walked the Lairig (that scorching May day in 1959 described in Chapter One) and as we trudged through Rothiemurchus Forest that glorious morning, talking about the supernatural, I said to Bob. "I met a ghost here once, or at any rate if it wasn't a ghost, then I don't know what it was." Bob watches with the keenest scepticism on anything I say, waiting to jump on the smallest factual error or logical fallacy. "Go on, Scroggie," he grunted, amicably aggressive.

First I sketched in the background. The 52nd Lowland Division, I reminded Bob, had been stationed in this Cairngorm area, the three infantry brigades in rotation, in the summer of 1942, when as a Lieutenant in the Cameronians, I had done my army mountain training with the rest based in camps at Loch Alvie and Loch Pityoulish. The object of this training was to prepare the division to take on General Jod'l in the rugged terrain of Norway, or perhaps merely to deceive enemy Intelligence that this was our object. Anoraks, boots, rucksack and all, nine Scottish infantry battalions together with ancillary arms, all under the bleak, grey eyes of Lieutenant-General Ritchie, the G.O.C. commanding, were to make themselves fighting fit for this purpose, so that the grouse that rose squawking from the heather would come to recognise in these incongruous disturbers of their peace, a force before which the Jaeger battalions of Hitler would flee in panic and disorder.

Sweaty, jaded and melancholy, the representatives of this force stumbled about in the mists of Cairn Gorm and Bynack Mor, too exhausted to comprehend the military business in hand, and what was left of their thinking powers concentrated on the girls and pubs of Aviemore, neither of which, as night came on and the storm rose, it seemed likely they would ever see again. "Fighting fit ?" was the jibe of these reluctant warriors: "yes, fighting for breath, and fit for nothing." Even the mules, to whom the N.W. frontier of India presented few problems, found the sub-Arctic uplands between Dee and Spey, the bogs, the boulders and the continual rain, sometimes more than they could cope with.

Under its burden of a 3.7 inch screw-gun barrel, one of these long-eared, short-legged monstrosities collapsed on the slopes of Corrie Cas, and no amount of cajoling, kicking and beating on the part of its attendant, a low-browed mountain gunner type, could persuade the mule to get to its feet and struggle on. I have it on the authority of Eric Southward, a tall, handsome, toothbrush-moustached company commander of ours, who witnessed these events, that the mountain gunner in question, in the last stages of exasperation, turned to his mate and uttered what I have always considered a supreme masterpiece in the economy of the use of words: at the same time, he flung his arms wide and shrugged his shoulders in a gesture of total despair, "'Orace," he said; " the mucking mucker's mucking mucked."

Had Ritchie tramped all the way from the sands of Cyrenaica to those of Loch Morlich, from the imminent hostility of the Africa Korps to that of the Cairngorms weather, simply to watch the reluctant sons of Bridgeton Cross huddled under boulders, and collapsing mules ? Had he been given the sack as G.O.C. of the Eighth Army only to assume the command of an outfit which could not cope with the Lairig Ghru, let alone the Bessingen Ridge, where General Jod'l awaited them with his schnapps, his cigar, and his superabundance of Teutonic military savoir faire ? By no means, for in this general shambles of incompetence, ineffectiveness, ignorance and reluctance on the part of almost all ranks, there were some modest triumphs to record.

Had not the Brigadier of the 155 Brigade, by iron determination coupled with miracles of navigation, got his jeep to the summit of Ben Macdhui, there to stand proudly by the cairn, his red tabs dimly perceptible through mist and drizzle. It is not recorded whether he ever got his jeep down again, or if its last vestiges still lie there among the boulders, now indistinguishable from the rusty bully beef cans which litter the summit. Had not one Sydney Scroggie got a 4.2 inch mortar to the top of Braeriach: true there were pack-horses and helpers laid on for this enterprise: and from 4000 feet he fired innumerable smoke-bombs into Glen Einich below to his infinite glee and delight, but to no discernible military purpose whatsoever. Perfectly futile as this enterprise turned out to be with regard to the War, it produced the one tiny vignette I was about to relate to Bob, and which, along with other incongruous trifles beneath the contempt of Ritchie and his staff, made these quasi-military adventures of mine in the wartime Cairngorms as memorable as any other experiences in my life.

Off-duty one of these Alvie and Pityoulish days, I found myself in much the same part of the Rothiemurchus Forest where Bob and I were now. It was evening, a westering sun slanted through the pines, the big corrie on Braeriach, Coire Ruadh, was prominent as it no doubt was now, and down on my right I could hear the thunder of the Allt Druie, swollen by recent rain. There was nobody else around, not so much as a Norwegian commando from Glen More Lodge, let alone those turbanned Sikhs and charcoal-complexioned Mahrattas who were wont in those crazy, mountain-warfare days to jingle on horseback through the remains of the old Caledonian timber with spur and pennon'd lance.

Alone, I experienced the whispering, timeless quality of a place which cannot have materially changed since the advent of Man himself in this neighbourhood of river not yet called Spey. I became aware of a figure standing on the path, or rather on a hummock of heather to one side of the path, and as I drew nearer I made out a tall man, as exotic in his way as any of those gaudy sons of the Indian sub-continent who now served the Division, inheritors of a culture in mysterious juxtaposition to our own, and in the last analysis dark and inscrutable. For the man, tall, stately and somehow ethereal, was dressed in the garments of some other age, black, shiny stuff, had a puckered cravat at his neck, and what with his smooth, silver hair and calm expression, seemed to stand there like some sage, contemplating in these quiet surroundings the deep, metaphysical question of mankind.

The most striking thing of all about this stranger, and that is saying something, was his complexion, a clear and pellucid pink and white, so that the beautiful porcelain quality of his skin gave an impression not so much that he was a real man, but that he had been produced by Doulton Ware, dressed in his antique clothes and placed there in front of Rothiemurchus to see what impression he might make on passers-by. I have since learned that a complexion of this kind is one of the marks of a perfectly healthy old age.

He stood strong and erect, and studied me as I approached with a calm and beatific look, something which went beyond mere intelligence, but rather a mental state too transcendental for me to understand, only observe. We exchanged a few words together, this seemingly post-Regency beau on the one hand, and a scruffy anorak'd, denim-trousered, clinker-booted hill-climber on the other, but I have no recollection of what passed between us, then shortly I pushed on up the track, my mind filled with a queer puzzlement regarding a figure who had inspired me by no means with fear but with a sense that there was something not quite right about it all.

In his presence I seemed to step out of one age into another, as if there on the wooded approach to the Lairig, the sun sinking, tits calling, and the Allt Druie continuing its immemorial course to the Spey, time had got dislocated so that all ages were contemporaneous, and I could as easily have found myself talking with Celtic holy man, sweat-stained Jacobite fugitive or grim cateran as with the preternatural impeccability of this antique, elderly apparition. I had a feeling that in the person of this stranger the past had materialised to have a look at the present, if only to confirm its opinion of a Scotland and of a world now beyond all hope of redemption, gone to the dogs. Turning, I saw pines bronzed by the reddish light of the declining sun, a stony track, ribbed with tree roots, descending between banks of thick heather, the distant Monadh Liaths, blue with the shadows of evening, and a silent Rothiemurchus untenanted any longer by any other than myself.

CHAPTER FIVE

When you have made enough height in Rothiemurchus to clear the timber, the track eventually swings away right, over wet peat, stones, sphagnum and swirling water, towards the crossing of the Allt Druie, and presently Bob announced that he could see a building, the Sinclair hut, as it turned out to be, standing on a heathery knowe

Outside the Sinclair hut.

in the distance. A melancholy memorial to the late Colonel of that name, this shelter was of fairly recent origin, and Bob and I were to discover in those four stone walls, two grim apartments, iron bedsteads and brave flag-pole, one of those shelters which have the advantage of providing a place where you can get in for the night, or take refuge in bad weather, but at the same time have the unfortunate effect of making the Cairngorms in general and the Lairig in particular not as remote and mysterious as they once were.

Change of any kind in the hills, especially where it is in the direction of the improvement of facilities, is something to be viewed with the utmost suspicion. The poetry of hill and glen, the metaphysics of gully and corrie, are better to be appreciated when you leave things as they are. It is almost better, from this point of view, that some should die for want of the Sinclair hut, than some should live due to the existence of it. Again, anything which encourages the influx of the wrong kind of people to the hills, those that think of them, for instance, as a mere training ground for physical endurance, must be opposed by those who see in them instead an area made for meditation, and those functions of homo sapiens which rise above the gross and the animal, and, in particular, seek an antithesis of the corrupting influences of civilization gone balmy.

On these grounds, the Sinclair hut should be abolished, and its blasphemous foundations resown with the heather its misconceived utility replaced; and yet I must admit, in the years to come, I was often to accept its spartan hospitality with a thankfulness quite inconsistent with this view of its unforgivable incongruity. However, I had not at this time made my first acquaintance with it, and as Bob and I skirted along past the outworks of the Lurcher's Crag, I reverted to the topic of the Fear Liath Mhor, from which the rest of my remarks had been a digression, aimed as all talking is in the hills at a psychological shortening of the distance involved.

"The most singular story of all," I said, "and that includes the terrifying experience of Norman Collie, is certainly that of Hugh Rankine, and I am indebted to this, as thousands are for their knowledge of the world they live in, to the columns of the 'Aberdeen Press and Journal.' " Whether paying any attention to me or not I do not know, but Bob trudged on over the rough footing, and I had no alternative but to follow him as best I could. Meadow pipits twittered, the sun, now getting high in the sky, beat down with torrid heat, and I proceeded with details of the story as I remembered them.

This Hugh Rankine combined three things in what seems at a superficial glance to have had the makings of a pretty crack-pot personal set-up: one, he was a communist; two, a Buddhist; and three, a baronet of the Scottish peerage; so that it was as Sir Hugh Rankine, disciple alike of Marx, Buddha and Rett, that we find him in the Lairig Ghru one day, accompanied by the good Lady Rankine, the two of them slowly pushing their bikes and lifting them over boulders in a way of doing the Lairig more popular in the twenties and thirties than it is now, the idea being to shorten the walking distance at each end at the expense of somewhat harder work in the middle. Jim Collie, of lower Tullochgrue on the Aviemore side almost comes into the class of eccentric by having regularly carried on this practice from the forties to the seventies, but at the time when Sir Hugh and Lady Rankine sat down for a breather somewhere on the descent from the Pools of Dee, the sight of two heavy, old boneshakers propped against a convenient erratic block would not have caused any surprise to some Seton Gordon, scanning the area with bird-watcher's glasses from the recesses of Coire Bhrochain.

I never saw Sir Hugh, and the picture of him in my mind is the exact antithesis of the fat, port-drinking aristocrat, but rather that of a small, shilpit crater, the fierceness of the Marxist in him tempered by the gentleman of the Buddhist, and the whole appearance, baggy and tweedy but at the same time debonair, embodying that je ne sais quoi of finesse and superiority which is the mark of those born in the purple. His lady I cannot help imagining in a large hat and flowered dress, as if she were opening a garden fete, but under the circumstances I realise this is absurd, so that it would be in a tweed skirt, twinset and sensible shoes at least that she sat there in the Lairig beside her eccentric husband, prodding the stones with her stout stick, as if anxious to be off again on the next stage of their laborious trek to Derry Lodge.

There, or near there, they would be able to get on their bikes, career down the last ten miles to Braemar, and if crankiness as to food was not another of Sir Hugh's obsessions, order the best dinner available at the Fife Arms, to be washed down with Chateau de la Lettre Rouge, 1920. At any rate, here they sit among the boulders chatting about Trotsky and Zinofiev, when the two of them become aware of a queer kind of music, woodwindy and pipey, which has started to vibrate in the air. From everywhere it came, those twangling strains, so that it might just as well have emanated from the bogs, boulders and heather around them as from the upper gully of the Allt Choire Mhoir or the echoing hollow of the Garbh Choire across the way.

It was not a trick of the ear, Sir Hugh assures us, as it is possible sometimes to hear bicycle bells in a Braeriach blizzard and voices crying in the waters tumbling down the cataracts of the March Burn. It was music, though of a disordered, inchoate kind, and it filled the whole of upper Glen Dee with its mysterious and other-worldly harmonies. As sometimes you do, especially if there is someone of exceptionally powerful personality around, Sir Hugh felt a presence in the vicinity of himself and his lady, and turning his head, he beheld a figure standing on the path down which they had just conveyed their bikes. The figure could not be said to be so close that it loomed over them, but it was not so far away but that the Rankines, astonished to the point of speechlessness at what they saw, could not study every detail of it clearly.

It was a man that stood there in the wild approaches to the Lairig, an extraordinarily tall man with almost disproportionately long arms and hands, and he was dressed in a robe which, starting at his shoulders, swept down, though girdled at the waist, till it ended above bare ankles and sandalled feet. The man's hair was long, brown and wavy, down to his shoulders, and the expression on the face, which had a kind of Indic cast of features, was at once calm and penetrating, the face of a man acquainted with inner mysteries yet at the same time master of practical affairs. The figure did not move, but simply contemplated Sir Hugh and his lady and their propped up bikes, as if meditating where these might fit into a cosmos far bigger and deeper by any yet cooked up by sage and philosopher.

Astonishment in the Rankines changed to awe, awe to a feeling of reverence, and shortly the Lairig was to behold a scene unparalleled in its long, dark history. In its day, Braeriach had gazed down on disbanded Highland mercenaries trudging homewards from the wars of Gustavus Adolphus, ragged of kilt and rusty of targe, with pistol and claymore. It had seen strings of highland ponies jogging along through the boulders, cargoes of eggs in pannier baskets on their backs destined for the markets of Deeside; heard the barking of dogs and the cries of the men, women and bairns that accompanied them. The same hill had observed with mild astonishment the advent of the first proletariat hill-climbers, as with dirty rain-coats and old army packs they sprang over the boulders in the general direction of Nirvana.

It had seen grey-bearded old packie-men pausing to pinch a flea or two between wet finger and thumb, by way of making themselves and their portable merchandise more presentable around the crofts and farms of Dee or Spey. In fitful flashes of lightning, it had witnessed Jimmy Ritchie cowering in his tent during the most prolonged and terrifying thunderstorm in the history of the Cairngorms or anywhere else in these islands; and it had smiled inscrutably to itself at the blind and panic stricken midnight flight of Norman Collie, pursued, as the venerable professor was to imagine to the end of his days, by the monstruous purpose of the Fear Liath Mhor.

Now, what this old hill beheld was the tall, serene, gracious figure whose description I have just conveyed, and kneeling before it in the stones of the path, their heads bowed and their hands clasped together, the persons of Sir Hugh and Lady Rankine, bikes, Debrett, Marx, and dinner at the Fife Arms all forgotten in the sweep of a vast and ecstatic experience. Buddhist theology asserts a group of beings, some seven in number, who are so far superior to homo sapiens as to be able to levitate from one place to another, live on air, and be equally happy immured in an iceberg or pent up in the furnace heart of Stromboll or Mount Etna.

Generally these beings frequent high mountain tops, and on the basis of some inscrutable rota, meet together from time to time, be it on Kangchenjunga or Ben Macdhui, to decide the next stage in the destiny of the world. Sir Hugh Rankine sees in the legend of the Fear Liath Mhor, misunderstood by the ignorant to be the Big Grey Man, some hint of one of those transcendental beings, momentarily or fitfully disclosed through some rift in the mists between Cairn Etchachan and Coire Sputan Dearg, or in some lull in the blizzard sweeping the desolate uplands between the Garbh Uisge and Lochan Buidhe. He sees in the mysterious footfalls heard by climbers, translated by their childish fears into some terrifying and dangerous apparition, the peaceful pacing to and fro of one of these demi-gods as it meditates in perfect isolation from the petty preoccupations of the world, mysteries too deep for merely human minds, solutions too abstruse for a wilderness of computers.

So now, in the boulders of the Lairig, and with the river Dee going about its usual humdrum business, Sir Hugh and his lady did reverence obeisance to one of these beings, his music thrilling in the air and his majestic person actually visible to their eyes in the light of day. "It was a Bodhisattva," says Sir Hugh, in the ephemeral scriptures of the Aberdeen Press and Journal, ".....a perfected man."

Sir Hugh, who had a smattering of various Indic languages, addressed this obliging Bodhisattva but elicited no information, either about the Fear Liath Mhor, or any other kindred topic, let alone any inkling of what was destined to happen to the Western Civilization in the near future. He tried with Hindi, Pushti, Bengali, Urdu and odd bits of Sanskrit picked up in his travels, but there was no intelligible response from the tall, robed figure, only quiet, mellifluous responses in a language, Indic by the sound of it, which neither our Scottish baronet, rapt in religious adoration, nor his good lady could understand. The unearthly music ceased vibrating in the corries of the Lairig, and there was only the rustle of the breeze in the heather, the murmur of the Dee, and the renewed twitter of the meadow pipits which, like the rest of nature during this extraordinary interview, seemed temporarily to have fallen silent. Opening his eyes, which he had shut for a moment in a fresh access of awe, Sir Hugh saw that the figure was not there any more, and that with the exception of the boulders, the grit and the heather, he and his wife were alone in the Lairig.

By this time, Bob and I were stretched out in the sun near an old plank which at that time spanned the Allt Druie in the neighbourhood of the Sinclair hut . The waters gushed past between mossy boulders, flies buzzed, cleggs settled on us in their silent, predatory way, and in the immediate vicinity some other representatives of homo sapiens, who had a couple of tents up on the boggy, green haugh, kicked up rather too much noise with horseplay and laughter. Yet how glorious it was, after the wait in Perth station, the night's journey by train, and the trudge through the Rothiemurchus Forest to be lying drowsily there with the heat coming down in waves on your body. As to my encounter with the antique and venerable gentleman of days gone by, Bob was obviously reserving judgement, but "Who would not be a Bodhisattva," he murmured, grinning, "on a day like this."

Somewhere beyond the frowning lip of the Lurcher's Crag now pleasantly brown and smooth in the Mediterranean geniality of the May forenoon, McLean and Scroggie luxuriated on the grass. Somewhere here abouts lay the remains of a hat of mine which had dropped off my rucksack no longer before than the October of the previous year. Padded, peaked, buckled and capable of being let down over the ears in severe weather, it was called my Afrika Korps hat from its resemblance to the headgear worn by those blond giants under the command of Rommel, whose duty it had been, a decade and a half before, to further the ambitions of Hitler and his Third Reich in the sands of the North African desert, ambitions shattered by Alexander and Montgomery at El Alamein, and to some extent hindered, however fitfully and reluctantly, by my cringeing pal, Les Bowman, then a sapper in the 558 Field Company in Tunisia, and perhaps slightly more formidably by another Scottish sapper in another Field Company in the same region, the burly and cheerful Bob Scott of Luibeg.

I use the word "cringeing" of Les, not because I want to tarnish the reputation of a gallant soldier prepared to lay down his life in the interests of the preservation of democratic forms of government, the picture of British warriors usually presented to the world, but because on his own free admission he spent all his time abroad, and this was true of the rest of the boys, not so much hungering to get at the throats of the barbarous sons of Fascism, but rather desperately contriving to keep out of their way as much as possible.

Chuckling reminiscently on that original trip of ours to Corrour, he related, as he often did, the terrifying events of a night in N. Africa when his unit was thrown into a panic by information that the enemy had broken through in that sector and were rushing towards 558 Field Company, Royal Engineers, steel hats down over bloodshot eyes and bayonets glinting in the moonlight, with the object, rumour was very strong on this point, of slaughtering them to the last sapper.

"What'll we do, sir ?" The cry rose from a hundred throats, and was directed at the C.O., who far from embodying the martial resolution of his race in this crisis, was darting about to and fro in his pyjamas, gibbering with fear. The satire of Les was always particularly envenomed when it was directed at the officer class, and particularly commanding officers. "Make for Algiers," was this craven's contribution to the saving of the men under his command, the words uttered in a high, trembling falsetto. Guns rumbled in the distance, flashes vied with the moonlight in the night sky, and these phenomena, which were a perfectly normal nocturnal occurrence, now lent fearful substance to the rumour which had swept the camp.

It was a case of "omnia ignotum pro magnifico" if ever there was one. "How'll we get there, sir ?" The response to the C.O.'s suggestion, for it was a suggestion rather than a command took the form less of a lusty shout than a concerted wail from sappers who could see their chance of ever getting home diminishing in a kind of geometrical progression as minute succeeded minute in the confusion of affairs. There are moments of inspiration which come to every man, based on memories long buried under piles of succeeding experience, and something new stirred in the C.O.'s mind, paralysed though it was by conflicting emotions, which seemed to have in it the solvent of all their terrors, the perfect answer to the unparalleled exigencies of their situation.

Pale, distraught and pyjama-clad, as Les remembered the image of him in the moonlight of Tunisia, the C.O. made a dramatic gesture vaguely in the direction of Timbuktoo, where Jupiter was a conspicuous object in the sky, gazing down with planetary indifference at a warring world below. The German advance came to nothing, even if it ever existed at all, but the walls of Corrour bothy now echoed to the C.O.'s words, exquisitely parodied by a convulsed Les. "Follow the North Star," he cried.

The rain came on, cold, heavy, steady as Les Bowman and I approached Derry Lodge on the return journey after that recapitulative night of ours at Corrour. It rustled in the pine fronds and in the heather, pattered on our rain-capes, and made little pock marks, always changing but always the same, in the puddles of the stony track. The skies were leaden, the top of Carn Crom was cut off by cloud, and away to the east and south was a distant rumble of thunder, premonitory of the garish flashes and rippling cracks which were to assault us in due course.

When the door of the bothy shut behind us, the latch making its characteristic rattle, I was not to enter it again till that blazing day four years later when McLean and I stopped off there to get out of the sun. My bootprints had long disappeared from the peat bogs by that time, the impression the weight of my body made on the plucked heather inside had long since re-asserted itself, and the Devil's Point, whose black crags, wet and shiny, glowered down on Les and I that first morning in May, 1955, had seen a blizzard or two in the interim, till it descried McLean and I, coming not going, step across sun-baked peat and enter under a roof which shimmered in the sun.

Now Les and I sat munching dates in the shelter of a gnarled Scots pine, and to keep off a certain moroseness, the product alike of dour weather and the imminent end of our trip, my saturnine friend, whose studied gloom was often relieved by flashes of exquisite comedy, was telling what happened with Ron Fraser and him in connection with a voyage on the good ship "Neuralia" when in the dark days of the thirties a complement of Scottish schoolboys and schoolgirls under some mystic provision of the Education Office were being inadvertently introduced to sin, as this was understood in various European seaports.

Fraser and Les had no business to be on this cruise at all, for they were much too old and had long since left school, but they crammed schoolboy caps on their heads, dug out old Morgan Academy blazers, and succeeded in getting themselves accepted as bona fide members of a party, with whose educational intentions their own plans were diametrically at variance. They seem to have got into a brawl with

Nazi soldiers at Keil, the consequences of which, if they had not somehow been smoothed over, might have swollen into a regular international incident, but it was not until the ship touched at some Norwegian port that these two reprobates, the one big, red-haired, brawny and aggressive, the other, slight, dark and by his own admission cautious in the avoidance of violence of any kind; it was not, Les informed me smiling, till they were on Viking soil that the big adventure of the voyage took place.

He paused, seeming to hear in the noise of the Lui as it rushed past us now, some echo of the turbulence he and big Fraser introduced into what might otherwise have been a tame and uneventful essay in young foreign fraternization, a mere peering in art galleries and museums, a dull catalogue of royal palaces, dilapidated castles, and places where eminent men were born or died or scribbled their unintelligible scores or manuscripts. These things were for the teachers, they didn't know any better, and for such schoolchildren who, from motives of boredom, unimaginativeness or sycophancy could not think of anything better to do.

In this Norwegian haven, appalled at the drudgery of all this educational stuff, Les and Ron slipped in the darkness one night, to seek out not the city residence of Grieg, or the flat where Ibsen wrote his plays, but the stews of town where in the glare of electrics, clouds of tobacco smoke and the thumping of an out-of-tune piano, they might discover something of more enduring profit. One moment they were staring with fake reverence at some floodlit Viking long-ship or antique, wooden kirk, their guide droning interminably on; the next they had vanished round a corner, swallowed up by the darkness, with all its rich potential of romance and adventure.

The Luibeg generator began to thud in the distance, the noise coming or going as the wet wind blew or abated. Les continued, lighting up a fag, and spinning the match away so that it hissed in a nearby dub. My friend, this Les, whom I had known some twenty years, was working up to the climax of his story, and needed a draw before he could be sure of delivering it with full comedy and panache. It seems big, hulking Fraser and he got into some boozing place, whatever they call these in Norway, and at the end of an evening of Viking wassail, though Les was never clear how exactly this came about, the ugly question rose, who was to pay for the drinks, the Scotsmen, who had perhaps made some inadvertent undertaking to this effect, or the assembled sons of Norway, whose looks, pleasant and affable heretofore, seemed suddenly darkened with vague menace.

There was a period of doubt, arguments and protestations being offered hotly on both sides, but in the case of Ron and Les there was a babbling fervour in their disclaimers to the payment, which was explained by one simple but terrifying fact, they had not an "ore" or "kroner" between them. The last of their cash had gone in a midnight Nap school only the previous evening with one of the stewards, a shifty eyed Liverpudlian, he was, and the third engineer of the "Neuralia."

The dispute in the boozer, it was agreed in the end, would be decided not by further argument, perhaps because of the language difficulty of which Ron and Les took full advantage, but by a trial of physical strength; and to this end, the Norwegians ushered forward their champion, a huge, blond, Viking giant of a man, sitting him down at one side of the table and sweeping aside the empty bottles and glasses in order to make space for the contest.

Where the "Neuralia" was concerned and its delinquent stowaways, there was no doubt who was the best qualified to step forward, but even the massive form of Ron Fraser, the broad shoulders and the ham-like hands, looked puny compared with this Thor-big antagonist that the heart of Les quailed inside him at the thought of the inevitable outcome. The two sat facing each other in the glare and the smoke, the blond mane of the Viking towering over the red thatch of Ron, the Norwegians gathered round to cheer him on, and as for Les, certain of a Scottish defeat in the bout of arm wrestling that was going to decide the issue, he was already edging towards the door, preparatory to making a bolt for it when the knuckles of Fraser's right hand came to the ground on the wood of the table. For it was about as likely, it seemed to Les, that he himself could beat Ron, as that Ron could beat this gorilla in a contest not in any way dependant on brains, but on length of forearm, development of deltoids, vital capacity of chest, and sheer animal determination and brute strength.

A meadow pipit twittered in the heather at the side of the Derry Lodge track, and Les seemed to study the noise in his most pensive and academic manner. Perhaps it seemed to my friend to embody in its little cadence that mystic je ne sais quoi which came to the aid of Fraser when his fortunes were at their lowest ebb, straining and shoving, his face purple and the veins standing out on his head, at that fatal Norwegian table, now so long ago. For when the knuckles of that big Dundee hand, invincible at this sort of thing up to now, were within a hair's breadth of the table, when that not inconsiderable frame, nourished on porridge from its youth up, was awkwardly and seemingly helplessly twisted sideways, and when a deep throated roar of Scandinavian exultation anticipated a victory on the part of their champion now as good as won; at this nadir of local Scottish aspirations, something stirred in Fraser which went beyond mere strength, rising to transcendental realms of will, ego, and inspired spiritual dedication. Call it the spirit of Wallace if you like, or Lady Katherine Douglas, or the 4/5th Black Watch at Loos; call it sheer terror at the consequences of defeat: but the fact is, even when the sweat of despair was smarting his eyes, Ron gave one tremendous heave, and to the chagrin of Norway and the infinite relief and satisfaction of Scotland, the knuckles of the Viking's right hand were seen to grind upon the table.

Les stood up and put on his rucksack, then helped me to put on mine. He was laughing uncontrollably, in the kind of half-synthetic way he had, at the recollection of his reprobate youth, his harum-scarum exploits with Fraser, and in particular, that boozy Norwegian night. "We walked out of that place," he said, "with all the suavity and nonchalance, as if we could do that kind of thing any night, and ....." beginning to trudge a little stiffly along the track ".....as if we had all the gold of Woolworth's at our back."

CHAPTER SIX

At the time when Bill Dye and I went off in 1958 on a long hard trip into the Cairngorms, Bill was at daggers drawn with his wife Dorothy, who sat furiously knitting and gritting her teeth. Bill told me the story as we lay in the tent. "I was going out, I said to look for some way of committing suicide. Her only reply was a vicious 'good'."

Puffing at his pipe Bill continued. "I stayed out quite a long time, and when I came back she was sitting just where she had been before, except the knitting had grown an inch or two. Sitting and looking as fierce and relentless as ever she stared at me and said 'I see you're still alive'. I said 'yes, the tide was out - and there were no trains'." From Bill's matter of fact tone, it was hard to know whether he was melancholy or in jest.

We had planned the trip across the Cairngorms to begin on Deeside and finish up on the Spey at Aviemore. Our first night from Braemar was spent at Luibeg bothy, which Bill and I were hanselling for the very first time. We were not the only wayfarers on the three rough miles from the Derry gate to the bothy, for as we trudged up the stony estate road in teeming rain, Afrika Korps hats sodden and army ground sheets dripping, a cavalcade of cars, black and ominous looking crunched downwards, forcing us to step into the heather to let them past.

"I hope Bob Scott isn't dead. It looks like a funeral cortege, doesn't it ?" It was not, for who should nod graciously in passing two of the most adventurous of her subjects but her majesty the Queen, Lizzie as she is called by the glen folk.

The convoy of Daimlers or whatever they were, guttered its way through the water-splash and disappeared through the dripping pines. "Rex habet curiam," I observed to Bill, "in Concilio suo in parliamentis suis." Bill, as he replaced his hat from his adopted loyal pose asked "What does that mean ?" at the same time humping his rucksack into a more comfortable position, giving me a tug to lead me onward.

Pedantry, Samuel Johnson observed, is the unseasonable ostentation of learning, and it is true enough that you have to soft pedal a bit with your friends, especially if they are acquainted with nothing but the handbook of engineering. "I don't know, but it sounds good, doesn't it," I admitted.

When we had skirted the brooding silence of the Lodge, then clumped over two broad wooden bridges, one across the Derry, and one across the Lui, we found ourselves in about Luibeg, hens scratching about, reek from the lum, and in by the row of wooden steadings opposite the house, and looking like a melancholy symbol of the decline of the West, the derelict remains of an old car. "If I had my way," I said to Bill, when we had examined this heinous blot on the scenery of pine, heather and hill, "I would call that car Oswald Spengler."

There was nobody around, no sign of Bob Scott or his wife, Margaret, and we climbed the rotted wooden step, creaked open the door with its clicky, latchy sound, and entered the silence of the bothy. A notice caught Bill's eye, one codifying the

A tame stag being fed by Bob Scott's wife Margaret

simple regulations of this howff, and he read out the various items, collect your sticks among the trees, the toilet is only for ladies, and so forth, then he chuckled in his usual slightly mordant way. "I see why your pal's called 'Bob' Scott," he said. Rain drummed on the tarry-felt roof, and there was a smell of old conifer firs in the stuffy little place. "How ?" Bill chuckled again, pleased with the astuteness of his wit, and anxious to communicate it "Because he charges a shilling a night for putting you up."

The bothy had a table, much stained with paraffin, spilt soup and ancient candle grease, and there were two or three chairs, some of them with the spells gone at the back and the deficiency made up with string. There was a little window, its panes crudely supplied with polythene, and shelves, in addition to dust, laden with the usual bric-a-brac you get in all the howffs in the hills, old lemonade bottles with paraffin in them, rusty prickers, a heap of green mould masquerading as cheese, a sinister bag of oatmeal with a date on it going back six months, beer can openers, festering old torch batteries, a battered lamp with cracked glass funnel, tattered magazines of picture stories concerning slant-eyed girls in kimonos, a visitors' book with pencil tied on with string, and innumerable manky, old bottles which in their hey-day contained the products of distilleries of Speyside, Islay and Skye, the breweries of Falkirk and Edinburgh, and with no especial predilection apparently for one or the other, the vineyards of Europe.

Dominating the bothy was a granite fireplace, so massive that it might have taken a day's labour in Rubislaw quarry to howk it out, with beside it an assortment of tongs, shovels and pokers, all big to match, a kettle with rusty interior, and an iron pot, dirty enough for a family of tinks and large enough to suggest it went back like the bothy itself to the days when the ghillies stayed there in the season.

We got out a candle and lit it, cemented it to the table with its own hot wax, and re-surveyed the bothy, now cosily lit with this yellow illumination. "Women and linen look best by candlelight," goes the old saying, and it goes for bothies as well. In the pale light and deep shadow all the anti-comforts of Luibeg took on a warmth and real friendliness. "Home was never like this, " said Bill as he laid the preparations for a brew and the primus began to purr. All that was missing was the brisk cheerful figure of its proprietor, Bob Scott.

Bob is a story teller par excellence, and to his door, remote as it is in the high hills, arrive all sorts and conditions of folk. Picture this scene on a day of windy rain and low mist. Bob is reading the People's Journal, Aberdeenshire Edition, when a loud knock is heard. He lifts his burly figure out of the chair, opens the door and takes, in a searching glance, a lad in cycling shoes and yellow oilskin cape, and behind him a frail racing bike propped against his gate.

"Aye, whit d'ye want loon ?" The answer comes in an accent somewhere between the Blaskets and the Aran Isles: "Might ye be telling me now Sir the way to the Larry Grew ?" Bob pointed where the river was pouring down from the hill in flood with nothingness beyond. "Bide in my bothy for the nicht, and wait until you can see your way in the morn." But the Irishman wouldn't be dispersuaded. He told Bob he had food in his pannier and his dynamo had a very good light. He'd just go ahead.

"Dinna be daft. Bide in the bothy," said Bob, laying on the difficulties of the pass in bad weather. But the Irish have never been easily dissuaded, after all didn't the Scots take their name from an Antrim tribe. So trundling his bike off, the descendant of Finn Macoul and Cuhulain disappeared into the mirk shrouding the pines of the Derry and Bob retired inside to tell his wife Margaret about the mannie who was insane enough to disregard his advice.

It would be three in the morning, black, wild, windy and wet, when Bob was roused from his bed by the sound of somebody knocking on his door. It was the Irishman who, in an exhausted voice, but not without spirit said: "This Larry Grew pass was a bit much for me in this wet so I left the bike against a pile of stones and came back down again to get into your bothy as you suggested." Bob didn't feel this was a time for head-shaking remonstrations. "Come in loon," he said. And as the lad stripped off, Bob put kindlings on the fire, put on the kettle for some tea and brose, and when the lad was warmed up saw him to the bothy with a couple of blankets.

Maybe Bob's last thought as he got back into his own bed was one that had come to him many times before when roused to help the exhausted in the night, "Some day they toon buggers might learn sense, but a' doot it."

Despite the lapse of time since I had seen Bob he knew me immediately, and as we offered him a dram from our diminishing bottle of Talisker, which we had decanted into a plastic container to save weight, we told him we were on our way to the Shelter Stone. The weather, he said had been fair hellish for the deer stalking, but he had to be out early in the morning for another day of it, then the benevolent despot of the Derry turned to leave. But not without a punch line! "Yon Irish loon wi' the bike, he wis never anywhere near Corrour or the Pools o' Dee or any o' that places. Folk found his bike on the top of Ben Macdhui. Good nicht wi' ye."

Bill and I were left sipping our Talisker, singeing our stocking soles at the fire, and reckoning, as thousands have done over the years that this Bob Scott, stalker, friend, and warm-hearted host, was a man in a million.

"I think, on the whole," said Bill, thoughts harking back momentarily to his domestic worries, "I'll just settle down here for good!"

But after many days and nights in the hills we were glad to be descending from the Lairig Ghru as darkness crept over the Cairngorms, leaving the mists and boulders for a silent Rothiemurchus and down to where the Spey slid blindly along to its salty destination. Our desire now was to meet people as we pushed into the glare of the Aviemore Hotel, and it was immediately apparent that we were not going to be disappointed.

"Hey," a farmer-looking man had gripped Bill by the arm, and pointing at me said "I think I know that man." If ex-Lovat Scout Willie Collie of Altnahatnich had not spotted an officer of "D" Squadron sliding into the bar with a hand on his friend's shoulder for guidance, many things would not have happened that night and next morning.

First there was talking about Arezzo, Alfero and Cusceroli, the sinister air of innocence that was the Gothic line, and the shambles of Gesso ridge, as fellow combatants relived their fighting days, and the ghost of Marshall Kesselring seemed to shape itself in the smoke of the bar.

Next as the alcohol began to take hold, and we were guided to victory by General Crerar, we translated these memories into action, creeping behind sofas, sniping round chairs and throwing imaginary hand grenades at non-combatant patrons, in an absurd masquerade of actual battle. "Hold your fire, Scouts. Wait until you can see the yellow of their eyeballs," was the cry uttered in paroxysms of drunken mirth.

When the clang of the closing time bell ended these adventures, down we went, led by Willie Collie through a black no man's land to surprise another ex-Lovat Scout heavily engaged in his grocery back-shop counting the day's takings. That was a mere beginning as the Lovat Scout element of Speyside was alerted that I was around as if risen from the grave.

The socialising was resumed next morning before the tea had come to the boil in our tent, as a head stuck through the canvas and a pleasant Speyside voice said "Well, well Scroggie, it's yourself." In the pawkiness of the words I had a mental image of the Rocky Mountains and a dazzling slope tattooed with ski-marks. I saw shells bursting on Woodpile Ridge, and the boys diving for cover into slit trenches, sunny Italy in the background.

In particular I saw in my mind's eye a sturdy figure in a black and white diced bonnet, the face below it, twinkle-eyed with a slow, smiling expression, with at the same time an air of resolution on it, Jock MacKenzie of Tullochgrue. "Buon' giorno, amico," I said.

Stationed for battle training at Glen Cluny Lodge, which then stood to the south of Braemar on the Devil's Elbow , this Jock and some fellow Speysiders, armed only with ground sheets and 48 hour passes decided to pay a visit home, direct by the Lairig Ghru in mist and rain. With tins of bully beef looted from the QM stores, and the confidence of youth, it didn't bother them that they had no personal knowledge of the route whatsoever.

After all, the Lairig had seen many soldiers under many circumstances, disbanded mercenaries making their way home with stern face, bonnet and kilt, broadsword, pistol and targe; weaponless, bare-headed fugitives with bloody rags round wounds, or fresh faced recruits leaping the boulders, lads destined to smell powder at Torres Verdas, Balaclava or Spion Top.

This was but another chapter in martial history. With Derry Lodge behind them and torches shining to pick out the path they felt they were on their way, following the river. Whatever hardships of this notably high and rugged pass they should be over by morning and looking down on the pine woods of Rothiemurchus to Speyside and Aviemore.

The rain was off when dawn broke. They were going downhill. They were over the pass, but the hills bulking black against the grey sky were totally unfamiliar. All they could see of domesticity were some scattered houses and a dark stand of timber. Now they got out the map to study how they could have gone wrong. They discovered they had never been on the Lairig Ghru. They had gone wrong at Derry Lodge by turning up Glen Derry. Said Jock: "What was below us was the Nethy bridge, ten miles further down the Spey from Aviemore. We had crossed the Lairig an Laoigh, an easier alternative than the Lairig Ghru, but too far to the east for us."

Jock now told me a few things that concerned myself, regarding me getting blown up in the war, and to make it more palatable produced a half-bottle, saying "Have some tiger's milk. It's the Glen Grant. It's dear, but you like the best."

On 17 April, 1945, cuckoos calling, sunshine blazing down over Romagna, and Bologna glaring white as paper in the shimmering distance, ex-Sergeant Jock MacKenzie patrolled below the forward slopes of Monte Grande, under orders, along with troop leader Curtis and some of the boys, to recce a new location for Squadron H.Q. Under pressure from a battalion of grinning Gurkhas on our left the Germans were falling back, and it was necessary for Squadron Leader Lyon Balfour Paul to see what his grey clad antagonists were up to.

So Jock, the tight-jawed Curtis and the rest patrolled forward amongst the baked earth, knocked-out tanks, ruined vineyards and shattered casas which comprised the landscape ahead.

As Jock spoke, I saw that landscape in my mind's eye as viewed at the time from the top of Monte Grande through my binoculars, sun-glare on the churned up bare clay, a dead mule here or there, a discomfited, motionless Sherman tank with drooping gun barrel, and through it all, the tiny alert figures on whose report depended the practical calculations of Squadron H.Q., and our immediate fortunes in the struggle to oust Hitler.

"The place was nothing but mines," Jock's voice broke in on my musings so that a mental image of the Italian landscape of those warring days gave way to one of Speyside again, the tent, the distant notch of the Lairig Ghru. "You couldn't put a foot down without looking. We couldn't believe it when we heard that a second patrol had been detailed to do the whole thing again, for we were lucky to have returned from the first one."

It was from this second patrol that Lance-corporal Kennedy, with an arm off, and a tolerably mangled W.S. Scroggie, both victims of Schu-mines returned to the Squadron on stretchers.

Jock finished his dram and prepared to get on his bicycle again. The cows of Tullochgrue were calling, his porridge, and the general business of life where at least temporarily the sword had been beaten into the ploughshare. "If you ask me, Scroggie," he said, vexed at my apparent disabilities like the good lad he is, yet determined to rub them in by way of condemnation of blundering military incompetence on the part of authority, "the whole thing was a damned piece of nonsense." There was a strong hand shake, the extraction of a promise to look him up the next time we came round, then the creak of an old bicycle as Tullochgrue went his way. "Sydney," said Bill, quietly and ironically savouring things, as is his wont; "how dare you get blown up."

CHAPTER SEVEN

If Jock MacKenzie and his merry men, instead of choosing the Derry Lodge road that fateful night, had followed the old carriage-way to White Bridge, their approach to the Lairig Ghru following Glen Dee would have been shorter and less complicated. If they had done that they would have passed within one mile or so of a lonely ruin called Ruigh nan Clach. Two miles or so south of that on the footpath to Glen Tilt is the ruin of the Bynack sheiling, once a good base for getting to the Lairig Ghru from that side.

A grand old man of Dundee hill-walking, John Ireland, minds the time when the Bynack presented a locked door to wayfarers, so that you climbed into the loft of a steading nearby, to sleep as likely as not, says John with a chuckle, with a pack-man on one side of you and a tramp on the other, for these hill passes were used by tinkers and pack-men whose burdens were not recreational, but laces, wool, buttons, knitting preens, thimbles of thread and what haberdashery could be carried from glen to glen, where folk still lived in places impossible to reach by travelling vans.

This steading fell down in time, and when Colin Brand and I dropped down on that lonely outpost distinguished by a few larch trees, snow on the ground and ice on the burn and the winter gloaming accentuating the remoteness and weirdness of the locality, it was to step over a ruckle of stones that had been the steading to push open a door of a Bynack no longer locked, but entering upon the last stages of its career, that of a derelict bothy for such as ourselves.

It was New Year's night, 1938, a day of sunshine, frost and dazzling snow in the Tilt behind us, and now when we entered that musty lobby through one half of a creaky, old-fashioned double door, and Colin struck a match, we found that whereas the three downstairs rooms were locked up and had furniture in them, the two bedrooms upstairs were open, and there we carried up our rucksacks, our boots clumping hollowly on wooden stairs, and settled in for the night. Lighting a candle, we surveyed our accommodation by its flickering light, our breath condensing in the frosty air, to see bare, dirty floorboards, a dormer window thickly furred with frost ferns, a rusty fireplace with swivel hob and wooden fender, low, sloping ceilings, and by way of furniture, if you do not count a long piece of snedded larch trunk dragged up there by some previous sojourners to make a seat, one bleak iron bedstead with no mattress, but only interlocked wires and springs.

There was no sound from outside, for the snow-covered trees were stiff and still, and the Bynack burn was locked in the grip of winter; and as for indoors, silence brooded, heavy and close, as if an old house, conscious of its impending doom, viewed the arrival of two clattering strangers with a slightly malevolent suspicion. The highlanders say an empty house comes to be possessed by a "bhuidseach", and this may account for the fact that you feel, in the echoing emptiness of it, that it is furtively watching you, but when we got a fire going, these feelings with regard to the Bynack were dispelled, and amongst the guddle of the spilled contents of our rucksacks we brewed up in the blackened old billy-can, fried sausages, then sat on the log to savour the delights of our situation, the residual knots sticking into our backsides, rime forming on the back of jerseys damp with sweat, and the fire burning hot against the knees of our breeks.

Home in the hills par excellence is any place where you can get a fire going and, here on the wintry threshold of the Lairig, merry dancers sweeping the starry sky with ghostly fretfulness, this Bynack sheiling, heretofore merely an alluding dot on the map and subsequently the sombre, silent thing of our arrival there, became through the magical transmutations of fire, the epitome of home not just to Colin and me, but to Mankind itself, you might say, in the wilderness.

This Mankind, Colin and I suspected, from which our remote situation that evening separated us not only physically, but by an immense psychological gulf, had seldom been healthy these past six thousand years, and at the present moment, on the brink of war, was in a particularly bad state. I studied my friend's face, now mysteriously shadowed in firelight, as he held forth on this topic now, the thick, black head of hair growing low on the forehead, the large, somehow visionary, grey eyes, and the puckish smile which could so suddenly transform the gravity of his features in repose.

He was a tall, lanky fellow, Colin, a clerk with Adam Will, the builder, and you could not follow his long, rapid stride over many miles of hill country as I had done, without being impressed that there was more in this brain and this imagination, this capacity of his to tackle any situation and master it, than was called for, or could ever be, in the high office stool he balanced on each working day, the sloping desk he polished with his elbows, and those dreary day-books and ledgers wherein lay imprisoned the soul of his employer.

Colin stuck a larch twig in the fire and lit a fag with it. There was a sweet, acrid incense in the fragrance it momentarily left in your nostrils. Yes, that chap Franco was up to no good in Spain, Hitler and Mussolini were a menace to the peace of Europe, and worst of all, the political set-up of which he and I were part seemed paralysed by inertia in the face of a manifest threat to its very existence, a threat far less due to the dive-bombers which had pulverized Guernica and the tanks that had recently swarmed into Austria, than to something in Britain itself, together with its irresolute allies, which made us ineffectual in exorcising a demon, in crushing an evil at its source, which bade fair to take over the civilized world.

The fire sparked and crackled as Colin gave it a kick, and in a corner of the room, faintly illuminated by candlelight, ice began delicately to skin our water supply in its old can. You could read the same sorry tale in the arts, was my contribution to the discussion, as Colin paused to shove a fresh stick on the fire. It was gnarled and springy, and sodden from the snow we had knocked off it outside.

In music and painting and sculpture, I averred, the rot had thoroughly set in, for all the old forms had been abandoned and everything just swanned around in a kind of blind aesthetic vacuum; and as for the productions of Hollywood and Tin Pan Alley, there was never a civilization better served with the materials of its own intellectual, imaginative and moral sclerosis.

These things were the index of the decadence of a culture which it was the business of the chap with the moustache and the forelock, as it was also that of the little, fat, bald man with the tasselly hat, to exploit in the barefaced interests of Satan. Caught in this enormous, retributive convulsion of history, what could two chaps like us do about it, one balancing wages and times in Small's Wynd, the other devising toplines and tailpieces in Ward Road, except perhaps sit round a fire here at the Bynack, winter stretching to the stars and the black hills beyond, and view the ramshackle stage of the world, not so much with horror at its tragedy, as with ironic amusement at the comedy of it all.

A fresh billy of water was placed on the hob, and Colin chucked a dead matchstick into it, a technique devised by tinks. A micro-film of turps, I suppose, spreads out from the matchstick over the surface of the water, and thus keeps the reek of the fire from getting into solution in it. "Anyway," said Colin, his fine face bright with the smoothness of eighteen; "I know what I'll do if the Germans invade." I was interested to hear his prescription against this disastrous eventuality, for John Ferguson and I, scrambling in Corrie Winter, had already made up our minds on this point. We would hastily organize a unit of mountain fighters comprising deer stalkers, rock-climbers, members of the Scottish ski club and stray youth hostellers, something roughly analogous to Waygand's Chasseurs Alpins or the vaunted Jaeger battalions of Hitler, and descending on the greyclad interloper from the Dreish or Craig Mellon, drive him back, in confusion and consternation, to the Munich beerkeller from which he so arrogantly emerged.

By God, if that sloppy lot in the Government did nothing about it, then the condottieri of Glen Doll would at least fight to the finish. "And what do you think you would do, Colin?" The fire suddenly blazed up, as if in response to my crony's enthusiasm, and he made a dramatic gesture somewhere in the direction of Beinn Bhrotain. I stared at the crack in the ceiling immediately indicated by his gesture, seeing in my mind's eye beyond it the whiteness of the snow, the blackness of hill, and all the peace, silence and profundity of a wilderness as yet neither jarred nor disregulated by the mischief of man. "There are plenty of deer in the Lairig," cried Colin; "I would grab a rifle and take to the hills."

Neither with a view to a reconnaissance of the ground in regard to this intention of his to withdraw there when the legions of Hitler moved in, nor for any other reason, did Colin ever, to the best of my knowledge, have his night in Corrour, gaze at the corries of Braeriach from the Macdhui side, or traverse the great boulderfield between Allt Choire Mhoir and Allt Druie. He was never, that is to say, in the position of the lad in the old Clova hostel jingle:

> "First I gae'd ower the Capel track
> An' syne I did Jock's Road,
> An' syne I did the Larry Grew
> Wi' Peem an' Shug an' Dode."

He was never nearer that haunting enclave of the inscrutable than Ruigh nan Clach and White Bridge, which peered at us through a driving flaffin of snow as we made our way down from the Bynack to the white-mantled timber of the Linn of Dee next morning. The Bynack burn runs into the Geldie, the Geldie runs into the Dee, and following these watercourses, in their successive increments of breadth and depth, I would not be surprised if I quoted to Colin, our heads bent against the flurry of wet flakes, the following piece on the majestic river towards which two days in the winter hills were now guiding us.

> "The Geldie, Ey and Slugain,
> The Quoich an' mair forbye
> A' stand the bouse
> This muckle souse
> Mak's free wi' on his way.
>
> Aye doon the strath he danders,
> Stravaiglin' like a coo,
> Till syne ae nicht
> He jist scales richt
> Intil the ocean, fou."

Bleak, white and barren, lonely as the moon, the Cairngorms vaguely glimpsed the back of us from time to time through lulls in the January weather; then we disappeared from their view along the snow-muffled tarmac of civilization.

Hitler dead, yet the world in general little the better, it was 21 years after that Bynack trip till I returned to the sheiling again, this time with that same lean, grizzled, ex-Popski's Private Army man Les Bowman, my companion of my first trip to Corrour as a blind man four years before.

Our object this time was Glen Tilt, and walking in from the Linn of Dee the wind gusting from the west bearing rain boded ill for dry breeks by the time we got to the silence of a Bynack far gone in dilapidation and decay, though sound enough in its granite walls and roof of Ballachulish slate. The windows were out, the floor boards were up, the laths showed through broken plaster in the macabre manner of an anatomical drawing, while of the furniture once locked upstairs, only a large kist remained, empty but for an old wine bottle or two, sundry discarded items of provisions, and a tattered jotter by way of visitors' book with stump of pencil attached.

There was enough rubbish lying about to get a fire going, shutters to blind vacant panes, and when we had fed, we lounged with our backs to the big kist, our knees hot from the blaze, drinking a dram from the quarter-bottle I had brought with me and blethering. Unhinged and lying on the floor covered with crumbled plaster, the room door had been lifted up by the two of us in consultation, propped in the oblong aperture in the wall it had once been its duty to close, and jammed in position with my big stick.

Names, dates and crude verses decorated the interior, pencilled on mantlepiece, pokered on woodwork, and lampblacked on ceiling with burning candles, and it was obvious that the Bynack, long abandoned by shepherd or keeper, still had that fitful life, that desultory, ephermal inhabitation, which is provided by hill-walkers and howffers, and which, in the fag smoke of Les and me, the fire which crackled in the grate, the candle which guttered on the kist, and the gear which lay strewn around, evinced the latest chapter in the epilogue of a decaying house.

It was this very decay, I suppose, which unconsciously suggested the topic of our conversation, for if it takes years for an empty place to deteriorate into the condition of the Bynack as it now was, the same effect can be produced in a trice by shell-fire, and in Les and me there were two characters sitting there with their backsides on the hard floor who had found themselves in corresponding accommodation more times than they could count in an Italy contended for between Eighth Army and Reichswehr in the now distant days of the War.

It was about two Kiwis, as I remember Les's Bynack anecdote, lean, tanned sons of the Antipode, who in sauntering a shattered Forli street, paused to examine what Les himself was looking at, a typewriter, brand new and gleaming in the Romagna sunshine, which sat among the ruins of a casa open to the sky. Not dressed on that occasion, as he now was, for the rain soaked Lairig, but in K.D. shorts, bush shirt and black, sinister beret with astrolabe badge, Les was in Popski's Private Army at the time, and as such was well aware that brand new typewriters do not sit in ruined casas of their own accord, not if the grey clad hordes of Kesselring, at any rate, had recently been around.

To anyone who had marched, however hesitantly, from the shingle of Sicily to the sun-baked plain of Lombardy, it was obvious this typewriter was not there so that an advancing Eighth Army could admire its beauty , but had been booby-trapped with a view to reducing the odds against Hitler by the death of some thoughtless looter.

These things Les now pointed out to a brace of Kiwi privates who seemed to him raw and inexperienced, and therefore not conversant with the wiles of a foe scrupulous enough to inject the very oranges on the trees with deadly toxins against their being eaten by an unsuspecting antagonist. Nodding in casual affirmation of what Les said, the Kiwis were yet unable to resist the temptation to creep into the ruins and try their hand at disarming whatever device the German sappers had prepared, getting the typewriter, and so return to Auckland or Dunedin with kit-bag bulging with this prize of war.

"I did everything to prevent them trying...." Les still seemed mystified, even at this long remove of time, at the obstinacy of human perversity " ..... except actually go down on my knees." Failing to persuade the eager predators with his importunities, Les got the hell out of it as far away as he could. A teller mine, for such he supposed was linked to the typewriter, is no fit company when it goes off for anyone with a notion to see the end of hostilities and rejoin his loved ones back at home. So the black beret of P.P.A. disappeared behind the nearby Dopolavoro, leaving the Kiwis to match their circumspection against the ingenuity of a wily foe.

Presently there was an explosion which rocked the vicinity and dirled in Les's ears with a kind of ringing clangour. A column of smoke rose in the summer air, debris pattered around, dust drifted in every direction, and the old sapper crouching expectantly behind the Dopolavoro nodded complacently as he recognised the symptoms of a teller going off. Les slapped his beret against his brown knee to get off the dust, then strolled back to where he had lately held conference with New Zealand.

Of typewriter there was nothing to be seen, nothing of building either for that matter, and there was no evidence, not so much as a stray spaver button, that there had been any souvenir-hunters there. Rain pattered on the shutters of the Bynack, wind roared in the larches, and in the sudden glare of the firelight I unscrewed the cap from the quarter-bottle and handed it to Les. "Obviously a case," I said, smiling at my friend's wry treatment of his story "of curiosity killing the Kiwi."

You do not let your friends get away with these wartime reminiscences of theirs without trying to cap them, even to the extent of making out as having happened to you what actually happened to other people. Les lit another fag, surveyed exposed laths, rotting floor and tumbledown fireplace with a lugubrious eye, and listened in his critical and not always kindly way as I launched forth with "Picket" McDonald's story, one relating to events which took place after I myself, blown up on my mine and carried from the field, ceased to take any active interest in the Italian campaign.

Picket, a quiet, clever pessimist from Torridon far gone in nostalgia for the old Highland ways, was patrolling around with his section somewhere in the wreckage when it became necessary to investigate a certain casa, the solidity of whose walls and roof were an outrage on the general dilapidation of other casas in the vicinity.

They did not go in the front door, a practice long abandoned by the survivors of patrols who did; nor did they enter by a window which seemed all too conveniently ajar: but got indoors instead through a skylight which was missing altogether, as if it had fled a house doomed to destruction sooner or later, if not at the hands of Hitler's Germany, then at those of some nearby Americans.

Cautiously, as behaved those men whose lives were sacred to the Democratic cause, the boys assured themselves there were no booby traps around, and selecting a certain room, settled in for the night. There were combustibles handy, chopped up sticks and the like, and in fact it looked rather like a Marie Celeste situation where the contadini inhabitants, pursuing the even tenor of their way, had suddenly fled in the face of some nameless menace.

Shuttering the windows, the boys laid a fire, and were about to put a match to it when Picket suddenly held up his hand. Either it was a touch of the Highland second sight in him, or experience of this kind of thing told him there was something fishy around; that there might be more than coincidence in those combustibles stacked so demurely where they were.

"Stop," he commanded, then getting down on one knee, keeked up the lum. Distant war grumbled outside, and the boys looked askance at their corporal, who now reached a hand up the lum and drew down a bag from the inside.

The bag which was bulky and irregular in shape contained grenades, schu-mine T.N.T. blocks, and enough explosive materials to obliterate them. All that was required to initiate their destruction was for somebody to light a fire which would burn through a string holding the bag by a nail. "We'll get in touch with the Germans," said Picket, placing the bag out of harm's way, "Somebody should get an iron cross for that," as he began opening a tin of bully beef with a bayonet, adding dryly with a knowing look, "me for instance."

Then Les began about the British landings in Sicily, when the Bynack shook to an appalling bang, as if all the grenades and teller mines I had been talking about had gone off together. There was no time for us to fling ourselves to the floor. We just sat there, against the corn kist in consternation and bewilderment till the echoes of the big bang died away through the derelict house. "It's my guess," said Les "that some American pilot is still trying to hit Cassino."

But there was no need for us to scratch our heads in vying with each other for the most fantastic explanation for the noise. It was neither a leftover shell nor a misguided bomb, but the room door propped up by Les getting blown down by a gust of wind and slamming flat on the bare boards.

Nothing mysterious happened to us that night in the Bynack, but just one month later a queer feeling crept into the soul of Bill Dye as he sat with his back against that same corn kist, and in candlelight stared at the flames of a corresponding fire. This is the same Bill who dropped into the Speyside end of the Lairig Ghru with me the previous year whose wife's only comment when he said he was going to commit suicide, shot one word at him, "Good."

In July 1959, Bill set out across the Cairngorms to get himself fit for a trip to the Norwegian peaks of the Jotonheim. Like McGinty's goat, he jist kept kniping on, pounding from Aviemore to Corrour and Whitebridge to the Bynack. Sitting at his fire in the sheiling, he took his ease complacent in the knowledge of a day's work powerfully done. Tomorrow, he reflected, he would hack on at full speed down the Allt Garbh Buidhe and follow the Tilt past the Bedford Memorial Bridge, Forest Lodge and Auch Gobhail, burst in the door of the Atholl Arms hotel, shoulder aside flunkeys with a shrug of his rucksack and down two big lager and limes before the door had shut out the noise of the traffic.

These reflections were followed in his mind by general thoughts of the hills, and these in turn, inspired by the moan of wind in the shutters, to a winter tragedy when five Glasgow hikers perished earlier in the year on Jock's Road. How terrible it must be, Bill thought to himself, the moment when you know you've had it, yet exhaustion and cold is supposed to be an easy death. There was something to be said for going as these men did, battling against the wind and whirling blizzard.

Where were they now, the souls that inhabited these fallen hikers, snuffed out of existence and found dead, face-down in the drifts? On the other hand - Bill glanced uneasily over his shoulder at a sudden creak of a plank - they might be wandering around their old haunts. Bill shivered at the ghostly thought. But after the stormy Lairig that day he was safe in the Bynack, and for all its subtle terrors of solitariness, he was glad to be there.

It was at this moment, among the graffiti on the mantlepiece, his eye fell on two names, so boldly pencilled that it might have been done for this very occasion. Bill, for all the practical engineer that he is, felt a chill at his heart. For in the names "FAULDS" and "DEVLIN" which stared sombrely at him from the flaked paint of the fireplace, he recognised two of the lads lately dead on Jock's Road.

CHAPTER EIGHT

What is meant by the term "spookiness" ? We all know, but what is implied by it is more of a mystery. Are there such things as malignant spirits which hang around places, giving them even in broad daylight a lowering and brooding atmosphere ? The Eidart bothy in Glen Feshie possesses such a presence, a ramshackle comfortless structure crouching in a boggy hollow, its background sound a muffled roar from the confluence of the Eidart and Feshie rivers nearby. It disturbs the soul more than other bothies, and gives you a feeling, especially in the gloaming that you are under observation from some pervading entity, menacing at best, and capable at worst of some terrifying enormity beyond the utmost grasp of sanity to comprehend or endure.

Is it on the other hand, merely some hangover from our early childhood which invests Altanour Lodge, silent, dripping and crowded in with queer, tempest-twisted trees, with an atmosphere which closely corresponds to that of Eidart bothy in dark hostility ? All people do not feel these things in the vicinity of a derelict Altanour or a squalid Eidart. For those who do, are they merely the prey of childhood fears inordinately extended into adult life, or is it the feeling in most of us that there is something beyond the bounds of normal life, something imperceptible to some, but which may yet impinge on others with a sense of just this sort of presence they perceive around such places as the mouldering walls of Altanour, the Eidart bothy with its wire-guy'd roof of rusty tin, unhinged door and uncaulked wooden walls?

Lower Geldie.

Let us suppose it is the latter, giving poor ghosts the benefit of the doubt, so that a certain spookiness some find round Lower Geldie Lodge, where Bob McLean and I bent our steps presently from Bynack sheiling, may have its origins not after all in the nursery, blamed for more evil perhaps than it really merits, but in some subtle posture of things as yet beyond the wit of man to comprehend.

I who am alive to vague, disturbing implications of Eidart and Altanour feel no sense of the supernatural in Lower Geldie Lodge, only a sense of illimitable distance, and the noise of the Geldie Water. Sydney Scroggie, the younger, on the other hand felt it an uneasy habitat by saying after drawing water from the burn "Dad, I don't like this place."

Lower Geldie Lodge was unknown to Bob McLean and I when we entered it for the first time in August 1959. We had nipped from the Bynack into Braemar for provisions, thus experiencing, as you do, at the height of the tourist season, a diametrical contrast between the silence of the hills for the hullabaloo of traffic, horns honking, tyres squealing and engines revving, which you get on that part of the Lairig route, now tamed and tarmac'd, between the quondam seat of Kenneth MacAlpine, King of the Picts and Scots, and the raging cataract of the Linn of Dee.

We looked for a lift along this populous stretch of road and Bob, studying the steel hinges at my left knee, the tin shank below this with rolled-down stocking and paint chipped off, and the battered boot whose heel-down, toe-up gait betrayed the wooden foot inside, saw in these melancholy reminders of the second World War a useful asset in the business of quickly getting to Braemar. "Get that leg more into evidence, Scroggie," he growled in humorous fashion; "put your worst foot foremost."

Meantime, the Dee rippled along beside us, a Dee which glinted in the sunshine and was oblivious amongst its algae'd boulders of two tattered visitors from the wilds and the sedate tourists who had come to gaze at it from dreary Blackburn and smoke-grimed Wigan. These waters had welled up from the bowels of the earth around Macdhui and Braeriach, received multitudinous increment from Derry, Geldie and Ey, and now ran down towards a Braemar where neither the sight of King Kenneth himself, risen from the dead, nor indeed lurching invaders from Mars with blue sparks zizzing between their antennae, would have ruffled their immemorial composure.

I reminded Bob what the bobby said in telling the two of us the previous May where there was a good pool to poach a salmon. "It's not people like you we're bothered about, who want to take one for the pot, but..." he went on, this amiable custodian of the law, to tell us of two furtive rascals recently caught in the act, together with the sixty salmon they had just howked out of the waters rendered lethal with cyanide.

Bob and I got our lift into Braemar all right, Kidrochit it was called before the tartan revolution of Queen Victoria, and in striking the stony road again later which leads from the Linn to the White Bridge, my bearded friend, who has a repertoire of such things, burst into a Gaelic tramping song by way of expressing the joy in his heart that the traffic at the Linn was now merely an incoherent murmur behind us, while in front stretched the bare wilderness which was more of a piece with his Mull soul.

Besides, we had plenty of grub again, and could look forward to a good fire, a good tuck-in and good blether when we got back to the Bynack. Bob broke off in the middle of "... And it's gaily sings the lark." Trudging on for a bit then chuckled, the pines whispering beside us and a greyness now over the sun. "That's the worst of these Highland marching songs," he said, rolling a fag: "if you're walking you haven't enough puff to sing them, and if you're singing them you haven't enough puff to walk."

It was on this return from Braemar, rucksacks bulging with bacon, bully beef and bread, that Bob and I reconnoitred Lower Geldie Lodge, with a view to moving in there if possible next day. We found very comfortable quarters in comparison with the somewhat dishevelled accomodation we had thought of as good enough at Bynack, glass in the windows, doors still impeccably attached to their jambs, a floor as yet unmolested by the depredations of pyromaniac marauders, a good table, benches, chairs. a hanging grate with sooty lum and dangling chain and hook, and a curiosity we had never seen before, either of us, in hill bothy or derelict lodge, a box bed.

Bob opened the doors, which were fastened with a swivel-peg and examined its interior, walls papered with antique editions of the "London Illustrated News", mice droppings and a six-inch mattress of old, stoury hay. Bob closed the doors to keep out the damp. "I think we'll move in here tomorrow, Sydney," he said; "I feel myself already seduced by that hay."

Go out the door of Lower Geldie lodge, as it was in those days, and you leave a kind of porch behind you approached by a stone step. There are nettles at the door, sign of soil enriched by generations of casual urination, and if you leave the building behind you and cross a small, boggy burn which crosses the haugh, you come to the bouldery banks of the Geldie, and a little way upstream, a long and tottering footbridge which spans the river in two strides, using a shingly island in the middle for this purpose.

There is no doubt there is a curious silence about the locality, merely accentuated by the low babbling of waters, and it is perhaps this silence which so profoundly affected the young Jamie Scroggie as to convert what would have been a pretty good walk through the hills at any age, let alone a sixteen year old. For him it became a mighty and unforgettable epic. This is what happened. The Duke of Edinburgh's Award Scheme forms the sinister background to the events.

The hills have many uses. The geologist prowls after rocks; the ornithologist scans them for birds; the botanist for flowers; the meteorologist regards them as a quarry for rare climatic conditions; the financier regards them as an area to be devastated for profit; the sociologist sees in them a milieu of benefit to mental-defectives or delinquents; the crook notes their possibilities as an area where he may rob wayfarers in bothy or derelict lodge; the psychopath hurries there to fulfil his death wish, or deliciously trifle with it in the name of artificial climbing; the army converts them to its uses as a battleground where soldiers can snipe at one another to their heart's content; the laird shoots stags there, hooks salmon in the rivers and on the moors hopes to kill record bags of grouse.

And now we have the Duke of Edinburgh's Award Scheme to help sort out the problems of a convulsed society, one part of it being a testing expedition on the hills with overnight camping as part of it. None of these uses, alas exploits what might be called an inner vision of truth.

Braeriach, Macdhui and the rest of the wilderness will leave the poet and the romantic in the silence with the philosopher and the metaphysician, to browse on the ambrosia which is invisible to the vulgar eye, to sip the unseen nectar to their heart's content, for nothing can ever harm their inner significance, degrade their perfection, nor in any way deplete their psychic inexhaustibility. And the Lairig will be there in all its glory, swept by the blizzard or bathed in the coral reflection of infinite dawns and sunsets, when mankind and all his absurd fatuities have passed away.

It was not geology then, or botany, or petty crime, or any other of these partial and superficial uses that drew Jamie Scroggie to the Cairngorms in the latter days of April, 1966, but the synthetic magnet of the Duke of Edinburgh's Award Scheme alone. Jamie did not know Scottish topaz from iron pyrites, or eyebright from meadow campion; but what he did know, from three experiences of it, was the route through the Lairig Ghru, and it was therefore in the role of expert that he was roped in by two school pals who had been bitten by the lust for gold, not as it can be diligently panned in the Tailor's Burn, but in the shape of Philip's alluring medals. And, in fact it is in the medals themselves, rather than in any benefits, dubious as these are in the means of gaining them, that the raison d'etre of this whole scheme comes to consist. Bronze, silver and gold, they are as idiot symbols of the craziness and topsy-turviness of contemporary society as the medals of that even crasser quatrennial folly, the Olympic Games.

However, these two school pals of Jamie's would go gong-hunting in the primeval wilderness, and when an itinerary had been fixed up which complied with royal decalogue, rucksacks packed and boots dubbin'd, everything was ready for a little expedition in which Jamie would not only provide know-how as to the tinky life, but also guide his pals from Aviemore to Blair Atholl via Rothiemurchus, Lairig Ghru, Dee, Geldie and Tilt, and taking in nights at Corrour bothy and Lower Geldie Lodge on the way.

Crested tit and crossbill would peer at them between the iron bridge and timberline; ptarmigan would catch a glimpse of three intrepid figures threading the misty boulderfield; sandpipers would acknowledge their passing in shrill utterances under the crags of the Devil's Point; dippers would interrupt their activities in the waters of Geldie as boots clumped the long, wooden footbridge and laughter rose above the swirl of the current; grouse would take stock of them in the heather and boulders beyond Bynack sheiling; deer startled by bawling and singing, would slip away from potential danger in the canyon of the upper Allt Garbh Buidhe; an eagle would stare down at three tiny dots from the corries of Carn nan Gabhar; chaffies and tits would not be oblivious of their passing in the timber at Forest Lodge. On the tarmac of the A.9, three days after the start from Aviemore, some passing motorist would notice Jamie and his two pals, weary, bedraggled and travel-stained, stagger out of Glen Fender road-end to collapse, perhaps jocularly, on the grassy verge. Having seen neither bird, beast nor fish by the way, nor any of the geology in which the route abounds, nor so much as a sprig of sphagnum or bog-cotton, let alone indulged in poetic visions, or philosophical or metaphysical speculations, the three would have nevertheless complied with all the requirements of Philip and his masterly scheme.

So much for the plan, and some imagined elements of its execution, but at this point two mothers stepped in, irrationally alarmed for the safety of their offspring, and where Jamie's two pals were concerned, imposed an absolute veto on their having anything to do with an expedition which female intuition saw as inevitably fatal in its consequences. Their sons were to bide at home, this was the purport of maternal remonstrances, and damn the Duke of Edinburgh and his crazy schemes.

Since the enforced defection of his two pals took place on the very eve of departure, Jamie was left high and dry on the Friday evening, more or less with his rucksack on, and certainly keyed up to a point where he would have taken on Edinburgh himself, if necessary, in a race to Ultima Thule. "You know the terrain, Jamie," I said; "why not do a solo ?" Jamie reflected upon this staggering notion.

In his mind's eye, as I imagine, he saw the gloomy notch of the Lairig beckoning him on; smelt in his mind's nose, the resinous fragrance of Rothiemurchus; and heard in his mind's ear the rushing waters of Beanaidh, Druie and Dee, as he had three times already heard them in a not unadventurous life. He saw the Sinclair hut on its heather knowe, and lonely Corrour bothy in the bogs under the Devil's point, both of which he knew well, and thrilled to the foreshadow of terra incognita as represented by such unimaginable places as White Bridge, Lower Geldie Lodge and the larch-girt Bynack sheiling where his father had put up so long ago that it was obviously not only in some other age, but in some other world as well.

He saw himself not only threading the boulders of a well known Lairig Ghru, scree clad Sròn na Lairig towering above him on the right, and the red, scraggy outworks of Macdhui on the left, but also reconnoitring his way down this Tilt place which looked so infinitely mysterious on the map, Allt Garbh Buidhe, Tarf, Allt na Crochaidh, then a friendly little square of timber defying the contour'd wilderness at this place called Forest Lodge.

He was a bit apprehensive, but in certain temperaments fear is a stimulus rather than a deterrent, and in this respect, as I well knew, Jamie took after his timorously indomitable father. Was not Bob McLean in the same class also as those who know triumph to the uttermost meaning of the word, only because they know terror as well. Jamie made his decision, some kind of vision of achievement or self-fulfilment dispelling the inertia which kept the majority of unawakened mankind from its Lairig, whatever shape that may take in the multifarious variety of human vocations. "Okay, Dad," he said.

Without any doubt whatsoever, Margaret MacKenzie is the canniest, nicest, kindliest woman who ever lived, and to a serenity she radiates around the house and policies of Upper Tullochgrue, she adds a twinkly, teasy humour, so that the picture a blind man carries around of her in his mind is a sort of da Vinci "Mona Lisa" superimposed upon a Giotto "Madonna" "I'll better get in the front now..." this, when you have vacated the seat beside Jock Tullochgrue in the landrover "... otherwise people will think we're not speaking to each other."

Added to her other charms, the old fashioned Scottish womanliness, the intelligence, the quiet, Speyside tongue, a never failing interest in, and recollection of, your family and affairs, and an untroubled certainty as to her exact place in the cosmos, is to be added to the fact that this Margaret Tullochgrue makes the best porridge between St. Abb's Head and Cape Wrath, a porridge by no means the worse for the cream she pours on it at the breakfast table from the mooing Tullochgrue cows.

"It's hard work for Jock and Donald on the farm," she says; "and they need the best of food." Donald is Jock's bachelor brother, an eager, cheerful, ebullient character, and in the division of labour at Tullochgrue it is his business to both deliver the milk around Aviemore and bring back titbits of news, so that Margaret can mull these over, attributing to each its exact importance, as she moves about her work in the kitchen, farm-court and steadings. Sandy is the son of the house, a tall stripling and easy and canny like the rest of them, and when some trifling perturbation coming from Sandy's direction momentarily ruffles the serenity of Tullochgrue, Jock winks at the company, then heaves his broad shoulders with mock resignation. "Who would be a father ?" he says.

It was in the bosom of this family, untroubled as it is by the sociological frenzies of our time, that Jamie spent the first night of his momentous trip, for Jock came down to the station in his venerable landrover, picked up the intrepid voyageur off the train, then returned through a yet unspoiled Coylum Bridge, to draw up amongst the tucking hens, mewing cats, barking dogs and lowing kye of Upper Tullochgrue. Here the rowdiness of traffic on the A.9 was no longer to be heard, a breeze from the Lairig sighed amongst byre and steadings, and Braeriach dominated the scene, snow-streaked and big, like a lowering symbol of what was to come.

And you have only to hear Jock pronounce this name, Braeriach, ripping off the "ach" with a fine Gaelic flourish, to feel you are meeting for the first time the hill as a living entity, with all its past history and implications for the future. Its silent, brooding presence, now corrie clear in the sunshine, now wrapped in grey cloud, is as much part of the life of Tullochgrue as all the MacKenzies who ever got their living there since Boney was on the rampage in Europe far away and Culloden was still a living memory in the glens.

Next morning, heather brushing his sump and boulders raxing his springs, Jock drove Jamie past lonely Achnagoichan, where the Nature Conservancy warden lives, and dumped young Scroggie and his rucksack in the vicinity of the iron bridge. "Here you are," says Jock, helping Jamie on with his rucksack and surveying the granite Cairngorms with critical eye: "From now on it's all yours."

Where covering the ground in the hills is concerned, there are various kinds of speed. One is due to a desire to get to your objective as quickly as possible, perhaps so as not to get benighted, perhaps with a view to bagging the best place in your bothy, perhaps simply to prove to yourself that you have it in you to put up a better time than the S.M.C. Cairngorm guide book thinks possible. Another kind of speed arises out of an opposite desire to put as much ground between you and your starting point as possible, this on the principle, operative in some temperaments, that to have more distance behind you is a more delicious feeling than to consider it the other way, namely that there is less distance in front of you. A third kind of speed, especially when you are alone and have a feeling the hills are secretly watching you, is a result of a vague, neurotic frenzy which willy-nilly impels your legs to their best performance out of fear, never rising into your conscious mind, that just to dander cannily along might be to lay yourself open to some nameless peril lurking in bogs and hiding behind boulders.

Jamie set off at such a pace from the iron bridge, and so resolutely kept it up, that it is safe to say all three kinds of speed combined in a crossing of the Lairig which can seldom have been bettered for time, as it can seldom have been worsted in that Jamie, hacking on over boulder and bog in a veritable dwam of concentration, can have heard nothing and have smelt nothing of what the Lairig has to offer in these respects, seen nothing of it except what was of immediate and exclusive importance in the business of getting from the iron bridge to the Corrour bothy as quickly as possible. While his eyes took in the track ahead of him, so that his brain was enabled to dispatch appropriate messages to his speeding legs, his mind was no doubt occupied with exciting fantasies of one kind or another.

He was a Jacobite on the run from Culloden, the dragoons panting on his heels. He was Marco Polo, making haste to gain the security of the Great Wall of Cathay. He was Peary, trying to outspace some widening fissure in the ice. He was Fawcett, somewhere up the Amazon, outdistancing, but only just outdistancing little, brown men with blowpipes. He was almost anybody but plain Jamie Scroggie tearing through the Lairig, for nothing so prosaic as that would have been sufficient stimulus to keep up his speed.

The timber of Rothiemurchus soon lost sight of him in the open bog-land beyond. The Sinclair hut had barely time to recognise him as a former resident when he was gone, lowping along the track where it twists up to the summit. The mists parting, Sròn na Lairig caught a momentary glimpse of him, then the mists shut in, and when it parted again there was nothing to be seen but the Pools of Dee, boulders, and a startled ptarmigan trying to regain its composure.

The Garbh Choire, suspicious of all human penetration of these parts, heaved a sigh of relief as he flew past. The Tailor's Burn, but only for an instant, caught his reflection as he jumped across; and it was only Corrour bothy, grey and brooding across the flats, which had time properly to make him out, for Jamie sat down at length on the bridge which crosses the Dee at this point, took a bar of chocolate, and proceeded to meditate his next move. His fantasies now in abeyance, he was alone with the screes of Carn a' Mhaim, the black crags of the Devil's Point, and the ripple of the waters beside him, as they swirled round boulders and between vertical banks of black bog.

As to the Lairig, in all its echoing bareness and starkness, it was far at the back of him now, and in fact it came as a shock to him that he had crossed it at all. And Tullochgrue ? My goodness, it might be in some other planet, strange and unimaginable it seemed so remote. The only realities were the surrounding hills, streaked with snow where they were not shrouded in mist, the immediate wilderness of boulders, bog and heather, the hard feeling of the bridge under the seat of his breeks, the dig of its bar in his shoulders, the sniff of damp breeze in his nostrils, and in one of his teeth, due to silver paper mixed up with the chocolate, an exquisite pang of neuralgia.

According to the plan, Jamie should have spent the night at Corrour bothy, and there it stood at some remove across the bogs, beckoning to him in what it seemed, in the vast emptiness of Glen Dee, a somewhat sinister way. It was an old friend, however, and Jamie amused himself as he took his rest on the bridge, by recalling a little incident which occurred there two years previously, when he had spent the night with his father and Donald, his tall, red-haired, dreamy cousin from London. Ramming some more chocolate in his mouth and stretching his legs, Jamie smiled complacently to himself in remembering the fire he got going in the tumbledown hearth. No-one, he was firmly convinced, given only wet bog-stumps and heather to work on, could possibly have got that fire roaring up the lum as he did, and in so short a time.

Certainly the thing had called for energy in collecting material from peat-hags near and far, but it was not often that old bothy had the pleasure of seeing sheer genius bought to bear on the business of lighting, tending and nurturing a fire within its walls, which in very short order converted the starkness of its accomodation into a cosy home in the wilderness. And perhaps not the least gratifying part of his achievement was the praises that were heaped upon him, not only by Donald and his father, who had seldom seen the like in all his hill career, but also by three amiable Glasgow lads who happened to be in the bothy as well, and now sat around with the rest of them, warming their knees, quaffing tea from chipped mugs, and companionably chewing the rag.

Jamie conjured up the scene in his mind's eye, the peaceful light of a candle or two, the shadowy corners, the assorted gear strewn around, the inferno in the hearth derived from ancient remnants of the Caledonian forest, and thought to himself that never was comfort, nay luxury, more perfectly embodied than in Corrour that evening. There was something in the contrast between the outside wilderness and the inside domesticity, he had noticed before which had a trick of transmuting the simplest amenities in places like this into good things compared to which the pleasure of the sybarite paled into significance.

It was a paradox often alluded to by his father, but if you wanted to discover comfort you had to come to Corrour. Perhaps that was the thing about the hills, that they stripped away everything inessential, so that what was left was pure gold. Jamie would ponder these matters some other time, but now he chuckled to himself as he recalled the rummaging noise which startled the little circle round his fire, the clink of a rusty can tumbling to one side, a thump on the threshold-stone, then a blundering clatter at the open door behind them which seemed to announce the arrival of some visitor with no uncommon notion of his importance.

Seton Gordon, the ornithologist, was too old and infirm now for it to be him. Perhaps it was the Nature Conservancy man, flaunting his giant powers. On the other hand might it be some tiger of the climbing world, smashing his way into Corrour with irresistible ice-axe. The company turned around, to behold not any Tom Weir or W.H. Murray, not the Nature Conservancy man with the last Caledonian pine across his shoulders, nor yet old Seton Gordon blinking in the candlelight, but an eight-pointer stag which glowered round for a moment, hacked at the door domineeringly with its antlers, then backed its way out, to be swallowed up by the night from which it emerged. There was a distant clink from another rusty tin, then the life of the bothy, as if nothing had happened at all, returned to peace and normality once again.

The plan had aimed Jamie at Corrour for the first night, but in the absence of his two friends, captives at home with mothers, Jamie was now at liberty to shake off the trammels of the Duke of Edinburgh, and do what seemed best to himself. It is difficult to get inside his psychology, for on the face of it there was no reason why he should not spend this night under that aluminium roof and between those dour stone walls.

Somehow or other, Jamie was reluctant to cross that bridge over the Dee, loup the peat-hags and open the iron studded door of the famous bothy, which had an empty and gloomy appearance. Within its dim interior what might not disclose itself to his eyes ? A green lady smilingly beckoning him in, the far wall visible through her ectoplastic composition; a troop of trolls cavorting in the darkest corners, or some crouching, hideous, misshapen figure, glaring at the visitor's book ?

There was no sensible reason for supposing these things. The Devil's Point loomed black over the bothy as it had always done, Glen Dee of which he was the sole occupant held no extra dimension of the occult or the supernatural. Was it not reasonable to suppose that Corrour bothy was any different from in the past ? Jamie could not be certain. Might this very ordinariness not be a trap laid on by malignant hidden forces to lure him into something worse than death within those seemingly innocent walls ? Jamie nodded complacently to himself at the ingenuity of this latter argument. The said malignant forces would come to realise that here in the person of this rucksacked traveller was no innocent abroad, no tenderfoot unaccustomed to the wiles of the spooks, demons and willies of the hills. He would therefore push on down the Dee. There was daylight left and to spare, he knew the track, such as it is, between Corrour and White Bridge, and perhaps in Lower Geldie Lodge, where the supernatural was not expecting him that evening, he might find that safe accommodation for the night which appeared all too doubtful in the case of Corrour.

The Devil's Point observed him get to his feet, chuck a stone or two in the Dee to see if they floated or sank, then, rucksack on back, head bent forward, and arms going like pistons, head south towards a distant glimpse of snowy Lochnagar. Word was passed on to Beinn Bhrotain, so that this gloomy mass kept watch on the tiny figure down below as it dodged boulders, lowped burns and sped along gritty straights in its headlong career for the granite slabs and sliding waters of the Kist of Dee.

White Bridge, in its turn, was alerted, so it was no surprise to its grey lichen'd handrails and eroded old planks when Jamie clumped over it, to disappear, his feet crunching on gravel, in the direction of Ruigh nan Clach, itself in occult receipt of the intelligence of his coming. You do not travel in the Lairig, it is easy to believe, without your movements being watched, your apparent intentions being communicated to all places which it may concern. So Lower Geldie Lodge, far from being ignorant of his approach, was ready to receive Jamie as he hurried over the landrover'd green haugh towards it, its door wide, its windows slyly watching, and its bare rooms loud with that silence which reverberatingly emphasises each drip, creak and snick, or pattering scamper of mouse.

This melancholy ghost of a house had been aware that someone was coming as

The Haunted Bothy.

far back as Jamie's getting off Jock Tullochgrue's landrover, had seen him against the mist-capped background of the Lurcher's Crag, skirting the grassy Pools of Dee, lowping the Allt Choire Mhoir, and had been advertised, in its queer way of his inner debate conducted on the bridge at Corrour. Thereafter the signals grew stronger, the Kist of Dee, White Bridge, and the crunching footsteps past Ruigh nan Clach, and now, as Jamie clumped into the empty room, Lower Geldie Lodge knew it had this fellow in its power. The trap at Corrour may have failed, but there was to be no mistake, this was the immediate purport of its broodings, on the banks of Geldie as there had been on the banks of Dee. It advertised its satisfaction in the shuddering shriek which echoed through the house in the act of Jamie wrenching the door shut. Now they were nice and cosy together, and as darkness stole over the hill and silence lowered around, the evening would reveal what it had in mind.

When the primus is roaring, and you are busy filling the billy, opening tins and cooking your dinner, the atmosphere of a lonely bothy, whether friendly or hostile, is not able to assert itself, either in the way of making you feel at home, or giving you an uneasy feeling it is time you got the hell out of it. It was when Jamie killed the primus, to use his somewhat homicidal expression, and the silence stole in under the door from outside that he became aware of a brooding something-or-another in the bare appartments of Lower Geldie Lodge, a presence as it were, just outside the door, an entity of some kind skulking on the stair.

The room he was in contained nothing untoward, as far as he could see, battered fireplace, bench, coggly chair, and table with evidence on it, in the shape of candle grease and paraffin stains, of desultory human occupation; that was all. Nevertheless, he had a persistent feeling that there was something around even there, something which had the ability always to dodge behind him, so that wherever he was looking, the thing was not there, so that it was always in an advantageous position to spring on him, or otherwise molest him, in some manner of its own choosing.

It was still daylight, that was something, but he could see a time coming when darkness would set in, and that was a time, it seemed to him, in the eerie shadows of flickering candlelight, when whatever it was in Lower Geldie Lodge would undoubtedly manifest itself, perhaps in some form so hideous that no-one could encounter it and retain his sanity.

His father had told him, he remembered, about the croft called Auch Gobhail in the Tilt, and in fact he had spent a night in it himself, though under very different circumstances from those in the story of Kathie McLauchlan of Forest Lodge, whom his father was quoting when he passed on the macabre ongoings in an older Auch Gobhail than the one known to Jamie. For the croft had been untenanted at one time, so that it was into an empty building, under the sanction of factor and laird, that an aged Skeenach woman from up the hill would move her belongings and take up residence, she and her bachelor son.

The glens-folk assembled to give a hand with the flitting, and the cailleach's belongings were trundled down in a cart, but there was no taking them into Auch Gobhail till the new tenant put in hand a ceremony which may have been common enough in the old days in Skye but was new to Glen Tilt. Taking a cockerel, she tied a string to its leg, then led it, strutting and squawking, through all the rooms in the croft.

"What are you doing that for, wifie?" asked the assembled glen when the cailleach and cockerel came out again into the sunshine. The old bachelor son was already humping an old rocking-chair in on his shoulders. The cailleach replied, as one well versed in the devious ways of the occult. The Kelts had not survived two thousand years between Uig and Elgol without knowing perfectly well that if you leave a house empty, for however short a time, there slips in a mischievous spirit, capable of many evil ongoings, and takes up residence there. "Ochone," said the cailleach, very mysterious; "it is to drive the bhuidseach out."

It did not take genius, Jamie reflected uneasily, to infer the possible presence of a bhuidseach here in Lower Geldie Lodge, and in fact, certain sounds about the place, otherwise inexplicable, could only really be satisfactorily accounted for on this hypothesis. In the absence of a cockerel, how could a man defend himself against supernatural manifestations. Could he sketch a pentacle on the floor with some detached piece of plaster; there was plenty of this around: and get inside it. He was rusty on the Lord's prayer, but was there not some formula of words he could mumble over and over again, and thus keep himself safe from the powers of darkness, or their agent on the spot if such there might be. Or should he attempt some kind of fraternisation with the bhuidseach of Lower Geldie Lodge, on the same principle that if you speak casually and soothingly to it, there is a good chance a snarling mongrel will not snap at you after all.

He was far away from any sanctuary. Linn cottage, where Bob Scott was born, good old non-supernatural Bob Scott, was a good puckle miles distant behind him at the tarmac road end. Forest Lodge, where the tilly lamp hissed and Willy and Kathie McLauchlan would welcome him in, was an immense distance ahead of him by way of Bynack sheiling, Allt Garbh Buidhe and the swirling, brown pools of Tarf. These latter places, in addition, he had no personal experience of, but only knew of their existence from what his father had told him, and from names on the map.

There seemed nothing for it but that he should sit with his back to the wall, concentrate fiercely on what defensive mechanisms he could think of, and somehow brave it out here for the night. It was at this point, however, as a kind of tramping noise echoed down from the attics above, that there came into Jamie's mind the thought of Ben Alder cottage. Instantly this Lower Geldie Lodge situation took a new and more sinister twist, and even as his mind pictured that lonely dwelling at the foot of Loch Ericht, the hero of the day's dash through the Lairig was gathering up his things and beginning to stuff them into his rucksack.

If anything like the midnight ongoings there, as reported to him by his father, were destined to burst forth into the Geldie, then he was going to get out of this silent, eerie, creaky place as fast as he could. Given some Dennis Fagan or Bob McLean for company, he could stick things out with at least an appearance of confidence: alone, there was nothing for it but retreat.

Any peat-hag, heather clump or overhanging boulder between here and Dalarrie, the McLauchlan's corrugated-iron cottage, was preferable to a Ben Alder situation, such as it rose dark and terrifying in his mind, transplanted to where he was now. Where was the spanner for the stove, his tinopener, his map. They were here just a minute ago, and who could have shifted them.

Since he entered that door not half an hour previously, self confidence had given way to doubt, doubt to uneasiness, uneasiness to apprehension, and now it was in a state bordering on frenzy that Jamie prepared to decamp.

Funnily enough, in this headlong flight of his from Lower Geldie Lodge, for such it was in effect, Jamie was running away from a mere chimera. What we imagine is always more frightening than what is, or as Tacitus puts it, omnia ignotus pro magnifico; and it was not so much what happened to his father, Dennis Fagan and Frank Anderson at Ben Alder cottage, as these things might recur in the Geldie, that now alarmed Jamie to the point of panic; it was rather the inference he drew from them, and most susceptible people draw from such things, that psychic manifestations of any kind, however harmless these may have been, always have it in them to turn nasty on you, to become a genuine menace to the physical person, as also to the mind itself, or anyone who happens to be around.

The trampings of booted feet, the rumblings of dragged furniture which reverberated in the building, and the prolonged, agonised human groans his father reported from Ben Alder not three years previously; these had been harmless enough, and, in fact, they had not been frightening at the time; but what if the agent behind these extraordinary phenomena had suddenly marched along the lobby, flung open the door of the room where his father and Dennis were, and proceeded to re-enact some ghastly charade not in a room at the far end of the cottage, but before their very eyes.

The packet of digestive biscuits which rose off the mantlepiece next morning of its own volition, soared across the room just under the ceiling, and alighted on the floor, standing on end, by the opposite wall; there was nothing terrifying in this at the time, though it gave rise to understandable wonder; but what if that same force which effortlessly elevated the products of Huntly and Palmer, had been correspondingly applied to the persons of Dennis, Frank and his astonished father. Could it not just as easily have lifted them bodily to hurl them one by one, or all three simultaneously, into the waters of Loch Ericht, or into the bottomless bogs of the Moor of Rannoch outside.

That such things had never happened, Jamie well knew, but might not this very immunity be a trick on the part of the supernatural to lure people into a sense of false security, and that now, here in Lower Geldie Lodge, was the moment chosen for the invisible agents of such things to manifest themselves in a barefaced and terrible display of lethal power. Jamie, fastening his rucksack with agitated hands, had no intention of obliging them, whoever they might be, in any such novel experiment. The bhuidseach could ensnare some less wary traveller; as for himself, whatever lay in store for him outside, he was getting the hell out of it while he was still to some extent at least in command of the situation.

The door shrieked again as he dragged it open, and Lower Geldie Lodge, robbed of its prey, saw Jamie fading away at full speed in the direction of the bridge. Silence descended on the old place, a silence, I firmly believe, broken only by sounds purely physical in origin, and a derelict Highland lodge was left brooding, if indeed it has any such capacity at all, upon its experiences in the past and its prospects for the future.

But the bridge was down, that long, rambling structure Jamie had been advised to look for, and the same spate which had swept it away still surged, foamed and swirled between the bouldery banks of the Geldie. Beinn Bhrotain gazed down unconcerned at this evidence of nature's casual destructive powers, and in the late afternoon light, a distant Beinn-y-Ghlo communed with itself on the southern skyline. Disturbed as he was with an acute attack of the willies, Jamie was in no mood to stand any nonsense from any barrier which seemed unsympathetic to his purpose of getting as much distance between him and Lower Geldie Lodge as rapidly as possible.

With not more than a glance at the remnants of the footbridge, he plunged into the tug of the spate, and thigh-deep at worst, made his way recklessly to the far bank, climbed it, then struck off at a scouring pace over the bogs and burnt heather towards the larches of Bynack sheiling. There was no question of putting up within these crumbling walls for the night, inviting though they were as he first glimpsed them against a background of waving larch-fronds, bleak hill, and grey, lowering sky.

What went for Lower Geldie Lodge in the way of invisible but palpable dangers must also go for this neighbour ruin, but to skirt past it, he had been told, was to strike the Tilt track, and there in the open country between Mar and Atholl he could shake off the last remnants of those claustrophobic terrors which had so oppressed him at Lower Geldie Lodge.

Moving with the rapidity which had characterized his progress all day, and with the knot of larches round the Bynack diminishing in perspective behind him, Jamie followed the bouldery track to the summit of the pass, legged it past the turf-embedded ground-plan of the old summer sheilings, then dived into the abyss of the Allt Garbh Buidhe, the river foaming down on his left, the hills crowding close around, and daylight manifestly fading into the gloaming of an April evening.

When he got to the Tarf, this solitary figure against the immense background of glen and hill, still deftly jooking round boulders and lowping burns, gloaming had faded into twilight, so it was less a sight of the river which advertised its presence than the sullen roar of waters thundering in cataracts, as they do, into deep, swirling pools below. There was a suspension bridge here, he had been told, which carries the track over the Tarf, and sure enough, glimmering in the last of the light, he made out the bank-seatings, woven wire cables and supporting superstructure of the Bedford Memorial Bridge. He felt his way on to it, heard his boots clump on the wooden planks, and stood in the middle of it, his hands grasping one of the cables and the bellow of the waters dinning in his ears. It seemed weeks since he quitted Lower Geldie Lodge, now far distant over the hill and withdrawn in darkness, months since he bypassed an equivocal Corrour, and a thousand years, if it could be estimated in time at all, since he eased himself out of Jock Tullochgrue's landrover in that other world of the iron bridge; and now, where navigation was concerned, he had come about as far as he could.

It was not that further progress was impossible: he had plenty of strength in his legs, grub enough in his sack to give the calories a fillup, and he knew from past experience how remarkably well you can get along in hill terrain even in pretty well black darkness. Nevertheless, without absolutely having to do it, he did not see why he should venture many unknown miles to Forest Lodge without a torch, a Forest Lodge where he was not expected and so would not be missed.

If he chapped at Willy and Kathie's door tomorrow, then that would be soon enough. Besides, where he stood now, the black water swirling below, the plunging cataracts dinning in his ears, and the bridge seeming to quiver with the violence of the spate; this precious spot in the darkening wilderness of the Tilt had certain advantages with regard to those unseen entities, some apprehensions as to which still vibrated in his soul.

"Noo, dae thy very utmost, Meg,
Tae win the keystane o' the brig;
There at them thou thy tail may toss,
A rinnin' stream they daur na cross."

The lines of "Tam o' Shanter" echoed somewhere in the depths of his mind, and Jamie now responded to them as one who gratefully realised that from the point of view of the supernatural he now stood in the safest place in the glen. Kelpies, warlocks, bogles, doppelgangers and poltergeists; menace him as they might from both banks of the Tarf, now shrouded in night, these denizens of the other world were powerless to get at him, immune as he now was in mid-stream.

There was something to be said for Burns, because for advice on this point, he would have ransacked the S.M.C. "Guides" in vain. A spitter of rain, laid on, no doubt, by the frustrated forces of evil, failed to dissuade him. Placing a groundsheet on the planks of the bridge, he tugged out his Arctic sleeping-bag from his sack, rolled it out on the groundsheet, and got into it, the hood pulled down over his face. For a moment the events of the day, perhaps the most momentous of his life, hovered before him in fitful phantasmagoria, then he was asleep, the Tarf sliding beneath him, rain pattering on his bag, and the hill world dark and inscrutable around him.

CHAPTER NINE

So much for a derelict Highland lodge, and its power to induce the young James Bewick Scroggie. At any rate, it was to this same Lower Geldie Lodge, having reconnoitred it the previous evening, that Bob McLean and I transferred ourselves from Bynack sheiling, carrying our stuff from the footbridge of the Bynack burn to the footbridge of the Geldie water in brilliant sunshine certainly, but in a tearing wind as well, very bleak and chilly, from the north-west.

Autumn always makes a first menacing appearance, I have noticed, in July, and this morning, bright as it was, no one could ever have accused it of being summer. Bob and I were pretty heavily laden, not so much with the standard hill gear, but with as much sawn-up timber from the Bynack windfall as we could lash on our sacks, so as to make provision against the barrenness of the Geldie in this respect. The timber round Bynack sheiling would have been planted when the house was built, so as to provide its lonely incumbent with fuel as well as shelter. As for the Lower Geldie Lodge, no such provision seems ever to have been made, and the last timber in that area, I dare say, was the natural Caledonian pines, whose evidence is confined in these parts to tree-roots in the peat. In times past if a red squirrel wanted to move from Spey to Dee by way of Glen Feshie it could swing from branch. Nowadays it would have a long walk on its springy legs and gey sore feet by the time it got to the Linn of Dee.

Waterlogged with three days of torrential rain earlier in the week, the ground was so soft that we sank above the ankles in places helped by our weight of timber. No trouble is too much however when a fire is at stake, and it was with some complacency we eventually struck the bridge over the river and headed across the boggy haugh to the red roofed Lower Geldie Lodge.

"McLean," the bothy seemed to say, "and Scroggie, or whatever your names are; you are just the chaps I've been wanting to see." The nettles round the door waved a welcome, the windows had a pawky glint in an affable look in their rusty faces.

There is nothing in the world to beat a remote bothy you have never slept in before, and I think both of us had an intuition that this Lower Geldie Lodge would provide not only above-average accomodation but that psychological je ne sais quoi which converts mere shelter into a home from home. "I don't know about you, Bob," I said as we clumped inside and surveyed the crude amenities of the interior, "but I think we're going to have a good night here."

At this period, my bearded friend Bob's lease of what might be called normal life was running out. The general lunacy of the world had for some long time irked his soul, so that there was a struggle going on inside him, whether he should quell his rebellious spirit, or throw off the subtle shackles which bind us to these conventions, and in throwing them off find some new integration between himself and some other world dimly perceived beyond the gloomy miasma of the one that hemmed him in.

Some people call this kind of thing running away from your responsibilities, or some such other unexamined, empty phrase, but I call it a transfer of allegiance from one set-up which is manifestly wrong to another which may or may not be wrong, and the only way you can find out is by trying. The big snag is that whereas it is easy to lie back and accept things as they are, to merge in the universal inertia; the opposite move takes superhuman courage, so that it was as much as anything else an out-and-out showdown between the forces of courage and the forces of cowardice in him that now constituted the struggle in the McLean soul. If his cowardice won, he would inevitably go with the rest of us pushing Western society nearer and nearer the precipice. If on the other hand his courage won, at least he might extricate himself long enough from the general mess to come back to it clearer in his mind by having withdrawn from its present trammels.

More was needed in Bob's case than those desultory withdrawals which satisfied me. It was not that Bob had weighed the Lairig in the balance and found it wanting, but rather that its remit was not global enough in scale. Bob's silences could be frequent and brooding as he thought about these things, forgetful of me sometimes where he would walk away and leave me, unaware until I bawled after him across the heather that his blind companion was not latched on by the thumb to his rucksack.

How wonderful, if not at the same time a little frightening, to have had an inner glimpse of what lay ahead for McLean; of the interior of a prison cell in Jugoslavia, the chair with its bound captive, the spotlight which dazzled the eyes of McLean, and the swarthy gendarmerie menacing him with buckled belt, the interrogators holding all the cards.

How it happened was this. Bob was having a meal in a Jugoslav home when the door was burst in and he was grabbed by a posse of police and marched off to jail as a capitalist spy. This was ironic to say the least in view of Bob's sympathy with Karl Marx, but off he was hustled, and presently, as a preliminary to sixteen hours of menacing interrogation, he found himself tied to a chair in a cell. Said Bob "I would have been prepared to tell them anything I knew, but they didn't know any English and the curriculum at my school didn't rise to Serbo-Croat."

Seven years after this incident, one by the way which had no international repercussions, and which only resulted in Bob being flung out of Marshall Tito's domain and told never to come back; seven years later, I say, there was a sequel to this incident, which occurred in no place more exotic than the A.9, somewhere between Dunkeld and Dalwhinnie. Heading for Ben Nevis in a car our possession of which was de facto rather than de jure, Bob and I picked up two girl hitch-hikers who stood at the side of the road in forlorn manner beside the bulky suitcases, which in addition to their sex is part of the stock-in-trade of girl hitch-hikers.

Bob and I had often been indebted in the past to drivers for picking us up on the way to the hills or back again, and we were pleased it was now in our power to reciprocate these benefits on two wayfarers who were obviously dependent on this form of transport for getting where they wanted to go. "They are obviously from the other side of the Iron Curtain," said Bob, his natural powers of intuition sharpened with regard to this kind of thing by two years abroad: "Their skirts are about as long as the Iron Curtain anyway."

Imagine our chagrin, perfectly altruistic benefactors as we sought to be, when the girls, instead of getting immediately into the car, drew back in some hesitation. Bob looks pretty fearsome, after all, with his big, curly beard, and there is something about my own appearance, bizarre and unkempt, which might be calculated to give pause to fair young wayfarers, thrown upon their own resources amongst the unknown ways and potential dangers of a foreign land.

Our chagrin, however, was not unmixed with amusement, since really there are no two less harmful fellows in the world than the McLean and Scroggie who now viewed these shrinking females through the hospitably open door of the car. "Come on," bellowed McLean with gruff joviality; "you're not in your dangerous old continent now. This is Scotland, and there's nothing to be afraid of." Somehow convinced that they were not after all to be side-tracked into the policies of Blair Castle and criminally assaulted, the girls climbed into the back seat, clinging nevertheless nervously to their baggage, and we proceeded up the A.9 at Bob's customary swashbuckling pace.

Bob turned out to be right in his assessment of the girl's country of origin. They came from Jugoslavia, and in particular from Slovenia, where they were students at the University of Lubliana, and were now for the first time having a look round some of those countries they had been taught from their childhood onwards to look upon with grave suspicion, as haunts alike of the capitalist system and that most dangerous of all political heresies, freedom to think and say and do pretty much what you please.

We got up a very pleasant little ceilidh as we drove along, Bob and myself exercising our repertoire of Scottish songs, and the girls, for their part, countering these with corresponding stuff from their part of the world; and it became obvious as time went on and we exchanged scraps of ethnological information between us, that Slovenia bears something of the same relation to the rest of Jugoslavia that in Britain you get vis a vis Scotland and England.

That is, the one looks on the other with feelings in which a touchy quasi-hostility is mingled with olympian contempt for a neighbour once so massively more powerful and infinitely less worthy. It was not long till we told the girls about Bob's experience in a Jugoslav jail, and laughingly assured them that whatever the deficiencies of the local political arrangements, at least they would not be thrown into the dungeons of Blair Castle on suspicion of being Communist spies. In fact, they could distribute as many leaflets as they chose in the forecourt of the Atholl Palace Hotel, and the only thing that would be likely to happen was that John McKay, the proprietor, would give them a free vodka or two for adding a touch of je ne sais quoi to the surroundings.

The girls were horrified, or affected to be horrified, at the menace proffered to McLean by their motherland. Did it hurt when they hit him with the buckles? Was his eyesight permanently impaired by the blinding light? "Of course," they said, and here their indignation was ludicrously Scottish in its repudiation of an imputed stigma on the character of the subordinate nation; "that could never have happened in Slovenia."

It is strange to think that this chap who now sat opposite me in Lower Geldie Lodge enjoying the fire and the water for his tea coming to the boil, this visionary figure called McLean, should have all that potential experience in him which was due to be realised in so many exotic and extraordinary ways.

It raised a question in me as to whether what happens to any one of us is inevitable, or whether after all we shape our ends, not destiny, and are free to act and choose as we will, to launch forth like Bob into the blue, or huddle round the comfortable electric-heater of an undemanding life.

Bob being Bob, had he really the power to deny the call of the wild, or was it willy-nilly he packed his rucksack to set off on his long trail to Khartoum, the Khyber Pass and to a self-realisation in foreign parts, not so much freely chosen, as forced upon him by some over-powering motivation in his soul ?

"What's for you will no go by you," is an old Scot's saying which maybe has some truth in it, and certainly it is tempting to see in your life, not something you have manipulated, but rather forced on you, with alternative choices as a mere allusion.

At any rate, knowing the outcome at this remove of time, I see my friend not only sitting as he did that evening, pouring out a small dram from our diminishing supply of Talisker, and as it was to be with him in the near future, astride a shaggy pony in a motley cavalcade winding along a track not dotted with its Luibegs and Sinclair huts, but only such hovels as serve a desultory trading caravan between Tibet and India.

These Mongol companions of his in homespuns were amiable and friendly, and had provided the shaggy pony, and had promised him a view of sunrise on Kanchenjunga once they had crossed a high pass. Day after day they had travelled hard, pony bells jangling, traders shouting, mist perpetually closing them in, and Kanchenjunga seemed as remote as the Lairig Ghru for all they could see of it.

Then one morning as he drank his Tibetan tea, butter, salt, sugar and green leaves all shaken up together with boiling water in a wooden tube, suddenly the third highest mountain in world was there, its snows and mighty rock and glacier walls rose pink, then the mist closed again.

Bob had crossed from the highest pass in the world to the plains of India. With me now he was embarking on another ancient route, by way of the Tilt where other horse caravans had gone in different times. Kenneth McAlpine, first king of the Picts had some kind of stronghold in Braemar, Creag Coinneach carries his name, Kenneth's crag. To reach the sea he had simply to follow the waters of the Dee downstream, and in three days he would be there.

Lower Perthshire was accessible by Clunie and Shee if there was any trouble in that airt. As for the middle reaches of the Spey, these could be kept under surveillance by way of the Lairig an Lui, Lairig Ghru and the Feshie, while due southward was Glen Tilt, the quickest way to the Garry.

These passes are rendered romantic and mysterious by these human connections going back to the first written history, and it would be a wonderful thing if you could combine the best of the past and the present, the past minus its savagery and its intermittent famine; and the present minus its lunacy, so that the life you lived could be at the same time sane and reasonably safe alike from slashing claymores and atomic explosion.

Bob and I, at least temporarily in this synthetic struggle for existence in this place, with just sufficient of civilized life in our minds as in our rucksacks, felt that it still comprised just a whiff of that old way of life as it was understood by the subjects of

Kenneth McAlpine. Bob was reminiscent that evening telling how it was when he got the job with D.C. Thomson's in Dundee which gave him the means to buy his books, his fags, his beer, and when there was nothing else for it, food. The Ordnance Survey had proved a cul de sac; the life of a vagabond had lost its enchantment, industry as embodied in a clock-making factory he had weighed in the balance of time and found wanting.

It was when he had seen an advertisement in a newspaper pleading for people to become journalists, not in the west of his youth, but east towards the rising sun so there he went, was interviewed in an antiquated office which still seemed to smell of gaslighting and Macassar oil and was given a job on the People's Journal. "I told the chap who spoke of toplines, titles, galley-proofs and the pulse of the public that I had never even heard of the paper, but despite the ominous truth, he gave me the job."

This lad of pairts and myself believe and disbelieve in a lot of things, but we share a passion for shedding all our clothes when the sun shines and we are in remote places. Whatever the church may have thought about it in the XV century, it is the pleasantest and most natural thing in the world. As far back as the latter decades of the XVIIIth century, my eminent forebearer Thomas Bewick, the wood-engraver, had a penchant in this direction, and I notice in his "Memoir" that as a laddie there was nothing he liked better than to take off his clothes, chuck them under some hedge in his native Northumberland, and career like a joyous, unfallen Adam through the woods and over the fields, turning somersaults, swinging on branches and leaping burns in an untrammelled ecstasy of joie de vivre. Quod licet Jovi non licet bovi, says the Latin proverb: what a god can do is no' for a coo: yet I do not see that what was good for young Thomas, still in the embryonic stage of his genius, should not also be good for me, and at any age at that.

Call it a subtle kind of voluptuousness if you like, but there is something about the feel of the wind and the sun on your skin which it is wrong for convention to oppose except in nudist colonies, as if to enjoy this kind of thing were some kind of shameful moral aberration. Shaw's black girl, when searching around for her god, came across the Venus de Milo. "Why," she said in perplexity; "is she ashamed of half her body." Again, it was a matter of outright hilarity to the Greeks of old that non-Greeks, or barbarians as they called them, should be so bashful when they were put up for sale in the slave-market, as they were then unclad.

The rot had well set in by the age of Carlyle, for in the passage in which he describes the execution of Charlotte Corday by guillotine, he makes out that the unfortunate girl, stripped of her upper clothes before the descent of the knife, still retained the blush on her face when her severed head was held up by the executioner. However these things may be, and whenever they may sort themselves out, McLean has the same attitude to nudity as myself, and in the solitude around Lower Geldie Lodge we were attending to various odd matters in the sunshine of a glorious forenoon as naked as the day we were born. The Geldie water rippled good-naturedly along, the twitter of meadow pipits was especially benign, a distant grouse sounded less cantankerous than usual, and all was easy, pleasant and uncomplicated as Paradise before the advent of Eve.

78

Out of the Laing

Far away from this idyllic, pastoral scene, and casting its grim shadow over the surrounding landscape is an establishment called Glen More Lodge. Putting on his winged sandals, Mercury could have nipped quickly from this place to where Bob and I were. All he would have had to do, in effect, is whizz down the Luineag burn for a bit, which drains Loch Morlich on the Aviemore side of the Cairngorms, cut through to the junction of tracks called Piccadilly, skim the Lairig Ghru boulderfield between Braeriach and Macdhui, soar past Corrour bothy, White Bridge and Ruigh nan Clach, hover for a moment over the rusty cans of Lower Geldie Lodge, then nonchalantly alight on the green haugh where, as it happens, on this occasion McLean was fixing a baited line in the burn and I was sitting on a log, thinking about nothing in particular.

As a matter of fact, to get out of Glen More Lodge is about the best thing that Mercury could have done, for this is a place dedicated to teaching people everything about the hills except what really counts. It is a kind of fascist training-establishment from which intakes emerge to conquer the hills and in so doing, according to the theory, conquer themselves. Absent is the poetry, the philosophy, the metaphysics, the dreamy dwam, if you like, which are proper to the wooing of the hills. A cowering Macdhui, an alarmed Braeriach and a scandalised Carn Lochain find themselves subject instead to a kind of criminal assault. Glen More Lodge, in short, represents a machination of the Devil by which he seeks to corrupt the last refuge of sanity with notions proper only to the general lunacy which surrounds it.

A good deal slower than our hypothetical Mercury, and, in fact, taking two days to accomplish what those winged sandals could in a matter of minutes, a flying column from this Glen More Lodge, unknown to Bob and me, remorselessly bearing down on the place where we were. With us, the sun still shone in caressing pulsations on our bare bellies, carefree meadow pipits floated down into the heather, their little song descending with them note by note in ecstatic trills; and the Geldie water, unaware of the impending arrival of sinister modern ideas upon the primaeval innocence of the scene, rippled along between its solid banks as if God were still firmly planted in heaven and all was right in the world.

The party from Glen More Lodge, driven on by bleak-eyed instructors, had the day before stormed the Lairig Ghru, swarmed down into Glen Dee and forced a bridgehead over the Tailor's Burn; thereafter to seize Corrour bothy, post sentries, and hold it for the night. Next day, they streamed down the left bank of the Dee, all nature fleeing in terror before them, burst through the rocky strait of the Kist of Dee, gained possession of White Bridge in a lightning swoop, and circling cagily past Ruigh nan Clach, bore down on Lower Geldie Lodge with irresistible elan.

The ultimate objective of their campaign was known only to sealed orders issued to their generals on their departure from Glen More Lodge. All they now knew, as they skulked warily round the corner of Lower Geldie Lodge, was that they surprised two denizens of the wilds, naked and defenceless, engaged in occupations blissfully in harmony with the unchanging laws of the cosmos.

As for Bob and myself, at a murmur of voices punctuated with ejaculations of surprise, we turned round, to behold in this temporary Genghis Khan role of theirs, some two dozen women students from the Dunfermline college of physical education. Some blushed, some turned away their heads, some frowned reprovingly, some chuckled to see the roles of Acteon and Diana thus reversed, while others stared blatantly, even eagerly, at manhood thus inadvertently exposed to invading femininity.

Some clothes were put on, some fraternisation took place; then this detachment of Amazons disappeared up Glen Geldie towards an unsuspecting Feshie. Things settled down again. We took off our clothes, affrighted meadow pipits returned, and the Geldie which seemed temporarily to have checked its flow, began rippling along towards its immemorial rendezvous with the Dee. "After all," I said, "The word 'gymnastics' is derived from the Greek 'Gymnos', which means naked." Bob had resumed his fish-hooks and was singing like a gruff linty. "That you being clever again, Scroggie," he said. "All I know is that we made their day."

Mice, it is pretty safe to say are delighted that the 20th century has taken so many people to bothies whatever their motives, so long as they leave behind some remnants of their grub. Even the Shelter Stone of Ben Macdhui has them, and it is pretty certain these whiskered, wee, timorous beasties are sizing up the contents of your rucksack with a view to burrowing into it at the first sound of a snore.

If they were squinting at us through holes in the skirting board to size up their quarry, it must have been with heavy hearts that they saw us hang up our kit on hooks before retiring into our sleeping-bags, our rucksacks inviolate as Mahomet's coffin half way between earth and heaven.

A Dutchman found himself in the Sinclair hut, the only other resident that night being a grizzled old lad with a Glasgow accent and had nothing about the normal hill climber in his appearance. Solemnly he warned the Dutchman about the mice.

"If you don't take out your wallet and put it on that shelf, they'll eat your paper money," he said, at the same time putting his own wallet there. There is no resisting the blandishments of the con-man, whatever you may think, and the Dutchman did what he was bid, and both men settled down to sleep. In the morning the Dutchman found himself alone. Fellow resident and money alike had vanished.

The Glasgow fly-man, if the story is true, went about his dirty work in a gentle, even humorous kind of way which reflects credit upon those of the criminal class who extend their operations even to such places as the Lairig Ghru. This was not so in what might be called the Luibeg case. The acts here were mean and treacherous.

Here at Luibeg we have a welcoming cottage, wood-reek rising from the lum, Caledonian pines, a bridge over the river, and a bothy that is almost a shrine sacred to climbers, where they can have shelter for the night and a fire, and good conversations and advice from the one and only Bob Scott if they want it.

Two strangers who had asked for the use of the bothy were in it, when Bob went to the door, told them that he and his wife would be away for the day, and said to them "Maybe you could gie ma hens a puckle corn, and help yourselves to an egg or two if you want." Away they went, and when the van rumbled over the two bridges and disappeared through the pines of the Derry there was only the 'tucking' of the hens, the calls of the tits, and the ripple of the Lui to break the silence.

On return to Luibeg in the evening the Scotts found their cottage had been broken into, money and valuables had been taken, and in a kind of macabre demonstration of motiveless violence, the hens had been shot dead with Bob's point 22 rifle.

In the eyes of the real outdoor fraternity, all Bob's friends to a man and woman, it was a far greater crime that Luibeg should be burgled than a Scottish regalia should be pilfered from Edinburgh Castle. Compared with it, to steal the coppers from a blind man's mug was a noble and high-minded deed. For did not this Luibeg and its bothy have almost the status of shrine, and its incumbent that of a jovial saint. Numberless frequenters of this wilderness country of the High Cairngorms felt personally involved.

From the Luibeg break-in there were two gratifying results, they caught one of the pair of low skunks who did it skulking around Fort William. He seems to have been a petty crook so paltry and inefficient to exploit the easy pickings in town, he chose to go for easier prey in the country.

Secondly, there was a demonstration of friendship far more multitudinous than Bob himself had any idea of. He was touched by it, and in particular by a sympathetic letter from a Dundee police officer. "Here's a pound note to you, Bob," it said, "And I hope you get many more letters like this."

At this Luibeg, as yet unviolated by despicable marauders, a few of us were gathered one October in 1959, talking about the best number in a party for safety. My own feeling is for two, one can always help one another in odd, unpredictable ways, fool about, exchange reminiscences, indulge in reciprocal sharing of delicate and private experiences, proudly discuss Plato, Thomas Aquinas, Marx, Schweitzer or some other author you have not really read; or over long stretches of boulder and bog enjoy that most delightful of silences, a companionable one.

I can remember whole hill days in the past when rangy Colin Brand and I exchanged hardly a word, yet all the time the companionship of each was indispensable to the other. On the other hand there is a charm about doing a solo in the hills which I have many times experienced in my sighted days not only on Macdhui and Braeriach and the remote solitariness of the Shelter Stone, but also in places as far apart as the Canadian Rockies and the Italian Abruzzi.

The beauty of this is that whatever the hazards, and there are really very few, it is entirely up to you. Pay no attention to them when they tell you not to cross the Lairig on your own, for this is the essence of the hills as a personal experience, not in an exercise in navigation or some other inferior aspect.

Three is proverbially a bad number, but there is nothing in my experience to support this, no sullen ostracism of one by the other two, no blows exchanged, and no difficulty in coming to unanimous decisions about what or what not to do. In rock climbing, while two are out ahead solving a problem, the third can tag along behind, with the spare matches and the fags. This happened, par excellence, on Gardyloo Buttress, Ben Nevis with Graham Ritchie, John Ferguson and myself.

In more recent years, when a blind member of the party reduces its effective number from three to two, I have found that while one looks after Scroggie, never I am glad to say leading him in to bogs and burns, though sometimes accidentally, the other can range about and look for the track, or shout back some melancholy information that the objective was further away than was thought.

CHAPTER TEN

It is interesting to reflect that what we call the permanence of the hills is only another of the manifold illusions which comfort us in a world where everything at all times is in a state of flux, and where it is the business of ourselves, in the interests of desire for stability, to suppose that it is not. You can never cross the same river twice, said the Greek philosopher, and in fording the Tailor's Burn, for instance, you cannot help but be aware that the water you splash through in your journey from Corrour to the Sinclair hut is not the same water as on the last occasion you did so, and will not be the same on the next; that the pebbles you stepped on last time have probably been moved a little downstream, others taking their place, and that all of them have had a little of their substance rubbed away in the meantime by the processes of erosion in which the Lairig Ghru, its surrounding hills, and all the high land-masses of Earth are gradually whittling themselves away.

Each spring spate brings down goodness knows what tonnage of detritus a little further in its journey to the glen below; each spring, in the thawing of the ice which has split rock from rock, goodness knows how much more detritus is furnished for its eventual destination in the shape of mere grit, in the oceans of the world. The permanence of your Lairig, therefore, is only an impermanence so gradual in its rate of change as to make no apparent difference to the landscape in the longest lifetime. Yet, in fact, there is not an item between Dee and Spey, if we are thinking particularly of the Lairig, which does not differ in some tiny detail as between one crossing and the next. Yet in all the centuries that man has used this pass for his purpose, except in a Black Pinnacle collapsed here, a big boulder rolled down there, there has been so little observable difference in the shape of things that it is understandable as well as convenient to call it the same place.

One item in this situation, however, which does most obviously change, and at a somewhat alarming pace, is the observer of it, so that the same chap who bounds through the Lairig in his youth is constrained to trudge through it in his middle years, and in old age, if he is still curious to see his reflection in the Pools of Dee, to make his canny way there, grateful all the way from Carn a' Mhaim to the Lurcher's Crag for dry places to sit down. We look at many generations of the Lairig, therefore, but they are pretty well indistinguishable from one another; the Lairig observes in stony silence many generations of us, not only unique and distinct, but also so transient as to appear in its geological eyes like a film speeded up.

To this comfortable illusion of permanence with all that it entails in way of beauty, interest and challenge, to this Lairig Ghru, I returned in 1962, and in the meantime, what with ascents of Ben Macdhui and nights at the Shelter Stone, scuttered about on its fringes, arriving at Lower Geldie Lodge again, this time in company with my cousin Donald Bewick, in the October of 1960.

The word imperturbable, if it had not existed before, would certainly have had to be coined in a desperate attempt to describe my cousin Donald. Up to this time, the high-water mark of this state of mind seemed to have been reached simultaneously by the Duke of Wellington and Lord Cadogan, who were standing together on the field of Waterloo when some missile of French manufacture came whizzing along and took away with it one of the latter's legs. Cadogan glanced down: "Me leg's off, " he said. The Duke glanced down also, and in his comment, "So it is," paved the way for that full flowering of imperturbability which the world was eventually to see in my cousin Donald.

Along with Gavin Sprott, whose wit and intellect, not to mention his resolution and hardihood, were an asset to any hill expedition, I was in Achtaskailt Youth Hostel with Donald, when the door of the common room burst open and a huge Irishman stormed in, clad not in the accoutrements of a hosteller, but in working clothes. In black darkness, howling wind and lashing rain, the An Teallach range rose nearby, the waters of Loch Broom surged angrily on the shore, and we suddenly found ourselves alone in the hostel with a lorry-driver who was not only drunk but crazy as well for revenge against someone who had just pinched the ignition key of his vehicle.

One moment peaceful and silent, the hostel now reverberated to the crashing of benches and tables as our visitor lurched about, as well as to the bull-like roars in which he vowed vengeance against the guilty party, whoever it proved to be. Looming over Gavin and Donald, he glared at them as if they might betray the fact, even by some barely perceptible motion of the features, that one of them was the chap he was after. "I have death in my right hand," he declared with great menace, holding up a full screwtop to prove it; then brandishing a corresponding screwtop in the other: "and death in my left hand." Apart from getting the hell out of it as quick as you can, it is hard to know what to do in this kind of situation. Conciliation is as likely to arouse an adverse reaction as hostility, and it is hard to strike an exact balance between the two.

This problem Gavin was discussing some days later with John Fielder, the landscape-painting warden of Carn Dearg Youth Hostel, and in particular made allusions to the danger Valerie Turner might have found herself in, the very attractive warden of Achtaskailt, had she been confronted by this demonic apparition at some time when she was on her own. John Fielder, apparently, knew the mettle of Valerie better than we did. "Valerie ?" he said: "she'd have given him a kettle of boiling water in the face."

Satisfied, though reluctantly, as to the innocence of Gavin and Donald, the big Irishman thrust one of his screwtops under their noses and commanded them to drink, and when they had complied with this order, he snatched back the screwtop and blundered his way out into the night. I was in bed when all this was going on, and rely on Gavin's testimony as to the punchline at the end of the story, one uttered by Donald, apparently, with such a degree of unruffled composure that the events immediately preceding, far from portending disaster, might have been a genial soiree at his cricket club. "That was a very nice beer," he said.

Mind you, it is hard sometimes to know if this imperturbability of Donald's is less due to an iron nerve and superhuman self-control, than to a naive and blissful incapacity to apprehend danger, even when it looms around in its most menacing form.

There was a gale the next day, and as it hurled itself at us from the Atlantic in violent gusts, Gavin, Donald and I took shelter behind the summit cairn of Bidean a' Ghlas Tuille, the main top of An Teallach. Climbing the hill, we had been blown off our feet several times, and I do not think I ever experienced anything like it before or since. Nevertheless, exposed as he would be to the full blast of the wind, and in a pretty precarious position, Gavin made up his mind to creep forward on his stomach and peep over the edge of the crag which here drops goodness knows how many hundreds of feet to loch, heather and bog far below. Flattened to the bare rock, and with infinite slowness and caution, he left the shelter of the cairn and eased himself over, peppered by small stones which were being lifted up by the gusts and hurled over the edge.

Vertically below, the view opened below him, like something seen from an aircraft, and for a minute Gavin took it in, the wind flapping his clothes, his hands tightly grasping the edge for security. Climbers had been whisked over cliffs before, and Gavin had no intention of sharing their flying fate. Satisfied, he was about to ease his way back again when out of the corner of his eye he became aware of an object beside him which suddenly appeared and perched itself on the very edge of the crag. Cautiously turning his head, Gavin identified the object as a large boot. There was another one beside it, and as Gavin's eye travelled upwards he beheld Donald standing there, his red hair all over the place, his anorak ballooning in the wind, and his trousers blown tight against the calves of his legs.

Now he swayed forwards, now he swayed backwards, yet somehow he miraculously preserved his balance, as if the forces of nature had not quite made up their mind regarding his fate. It was as if Gavin did not exist, or that the reason for his friend's lying on his stomach did not penetrate Donald's mind. As if there was only the height of a Hornsea kerbstone below him, Donald stood there with his hands in his pockets, serenely surveying the beauties of nature as spread out for his benefit. Seeming to catch sight of Gavin, he gave him a puzzled glance, then strolled back to the summit cairn with all the casualness of a man to whom a force nine gale is of no more consequence than a zephyr in spring. Such then is the imperturbability, or whatever you think it may be, of my cousin Donald.

So by the way of Harper's barn in Glen Clova, Sandy Hillocks hut, Lochend bothy in Glen Muick, Luibeg and empty Achearie house in Glen Ey, myself and this Donald, six foot three, with thick, carroty-red hair, and plunged from time to time in a mood of impenetrable abstraction, arrived at Lower Geldie Lodge as the light was fading at the end of a bleak autumn day. Beinn Bhrotain, dark and menacing as ever, stood in its accustomed place, wet moorland stretched away as usual to the distant Beinn-y-Ghlo, and the Geldie water ran along to the Dee, seemingly in blank ignorance of the fact that it was fourteen months since the one-legged blind man was there before.

The hills in general pay very little attention to their visitors, preferring their own inscrutable company. We had seen Geordie Grant, the shepherd, that day, whose dogs, pushbike, skeppit bonnet, Aberdeenshire tongue, and puffed pipe of black baccy were usually a feature of the Glen Ey scene; Alex Dempster had hailed us at the Knock, reminding us, this Highland-spoken deer stalker from Sutherland, that there

Bob Scott's country. From Derry Cairngorm looking down onto Glen Lui Beg's ancient pines

was another great friend to walkers and climbers on the fringes of the Lairig, a kindly, humorous man who would not see you stuck if his cosy bothy could keep the wind and rain off you for the night; Mrs McDougal of Bel-an-Ey cottage, Inverey, warden of the mini Youth Hostel next door, had entertained us with tea, pieces and various ragtags of information regarding a locality which her amiable presence has graced for many a year: and, of course, at Luibeg itself, the great Bob Scott had again embraced me and a companion with all the warmth and vigour of his cheery personality.

Perhaps this was the occasion when he told us the story about the chap who was at great expense to take the fishing for a fortnight of some Irish stream. Not a fish did he catch, and it was on the evening of his departure that he addressed the ghillie who had been with him all the fortnight. "Patrick," he said; "I know you have your home and garden to attend to, but may be you could just come out with me this evening and see if we can't get a fish in spite of everything. You will be handsomely requited." The ghillie agreed and what should happen but between them they landed a 15 pound salmon, laying it beside them at midnight on the bank of the stream. The gent gazed down at it. "Do you know, Patrick," he said; "this fish has cost me a hundred pounds," The ghillie paused in the act of folding up his landing net. "Mother of God, sir," he said; "and isn't it a good job you didn't catch any more."

Or maybe, the fire in the bothy crackling into life and the primus roaring, it was on this occasion he told the story, his eyes twinkling as ever, of the full-scale rescue operation he mounted to bring in a lad lying unconscious in the Lairig. What with the R.A.F. mountain-rescue team, police, tracker dogs and local volunteers, the lad was got into Luibeg cottage at length and laid on a bed. Here he regained consciousness, asked for a bottle of pills to be brought him from the bothy where he had left some of his things, swallowed one of the pills, and after a while got on his feet, as right as rain. "There was nae need for a' the stushy ava'," said Bob, alluding to the vast disruption of normal life which is the effect of a mountain-rescue operation. "If someone had jist telt us he was a diabetic, jist the ae lad carrying a peel wad hae been a' that wis wantit."

Far from the Belisha beacons, zebra crossings, street names and other aids to navigation in his native Hornsea, Donald showed signs of disorientation in hill surroundings, so that I had to exercise constant vigilance to make sure we were going the right way, not drifting away down the Tilt, for instance, on this present occasion, or inadvertently taking the path at White Bridge to Corrour bothy, so it was with some relief that the echo of our voices coming back to us indicated we were approaching what could be nothing other than Lower Geldie Lodge. The map seemed to be of little use to Donald, all those funny lines and queer Gaelic names, and it was only by constant cross-examination as to what he could see in the landscape around him that I could ever be sure we were on the right road. This information, conscious of his deficiencies as a navigator, Donald supplied with characteristic good humour and aplomb, so that between the two of us, Donald supplying the eyes and myself a knowledge of the ground, the two of us never made many mistakes which were not immediately retrievable.

Nevertheless, it was always with a sense of relief, of relaxation of tension, that I arrived with him at any objective in the hills; and now, as the door of Lower Geldie Lodge screeched open, I entered into the silence of the building with a sense of spiritual release akin to that of any Catholic after confession. The minor anxieties which thus arose out of a trip with Donald were over, and far from having to bed down on some unknown patch of heather for the night, we were safe in the rude hospitality of a place I knew. The charm of Bob McLean was that he liked to get lost deliberately; a terrifying drawback of Donald was that he might lose us both accidentally.

Our arrival at the Lodge pretty well coincided with the drawing-in of darkness. Venus had made her appearance, trembling in the west, the hills had withdrawn in their grey plaid of mist, and the ultimate condition of a good day in the hills was therefore satisfied, that you should arrive at your destination in the last of the light. That your trip should start in darkness and end in darkness is somehow of a piece with the aesthetic of the thing. We got a candle going and stuck it on the table; Donald fetched water in brimming billy cans, and shortly the primus stove was roaring with its immediate overtures of unstinted friendliness and its promise of eventual hot grub and tea.

The modern gas stoves may be all very well, and they have some modest place in the hill scene, but for the companionableness of its noise, its ferocious efficiency, there is nothing like the primus, these and the nostalgic aroma of its fuel which hangs about it like the happy miasma from a thousand previous adventures in the wilds. You know the tea is ready by a delicious oriental fragrance which begins to diffuse itself in the musty atmosphere of your bothy, and Donald was about to take the billy off the can when the door opened and two figures with rucksacks came in. What they saw apparently was a Highland laird and his retainer, fallen on evil days certainly, but still eking out some sort of existence in their ancestral stamping grounds despite the rigours of taxation and their losing battle against the proletariat.

Gone were the Rembrants from the walls, the Chippendale furniture, and the priceless bric-a-brac from the four corners of the world, all put under the hammer at Sotheby's to stave off bankruptcy. The Adams fireplace, like the Sheraton side-board and Louis Quinze table, had been broken up for firewood. All that was left of the glory that had been were two tatteredemalion figures making the most of it with candle and stove in the melancholy ruins of a life once as gracious and civilized as the Palace of Holyrood House. What the strangers said, therefore, was deferential, as designed not to offend the susceptibilities of great landowners now fallen on evil days, to give them their place as in the palmy days of old, "May we come in ?" they asked.

With regard to a drink of water, we learned at school with awe that when this was offered to Sir Philip Sydney as he lay wounded on the field of Zutphen, he indicated another casualty moaning nearby. "Give it to him," he is reported to have said: "His need is greater than mine." When Donald and I heard from our visitors, or as they would have it, our guests, that they had walked that day, and at a great pace, from Strath Tummel Youth Hostel to Lower Geldic Lodge; heard this, and compared their monumental march with our own petty saunter from Altanour, we lowered our lips from the brimming mugs of tea we had been about to start drinking, and handed them instead to two wayfarers in whom we recognised the supremest dedication to their calling, not to mention a need for this tea manifestly greater than our own. Gulping it down, one with a commando beret and para-military gear, the other more orthodox in his accoutrements, they gave us a rapid sketch of their adventures that day, then asked how far it might be to Mrs McDougal's mini Youth Hostel at In-verey, this being the objective, in their merciless mortification of the flesh, which they had set themselves.

Now, it is nice to have company in your bothy, apart from yourselves, and I did not like the thought of these two fellows, who struck me as sterling characters, dis-appearing for ever from my life after so short an acquaintance. Certainly they had no sleeping-bags, but "Listen," I said, "there's a box-bed in the wall there, and plenty of hay, so why not stay here for the night ?" Roger Titball was the name of the chap in the commando beret, a chunky, amiably aggressive character, the other David Milne, a quiet, less obtrusive personality; both of them Cambridge undergraduates.

They conferred over my suggestion, the primus brewing more tea, and decided to comply with it. By this time they had recognised in Lower Geldie Lodge the derelict, old building which was all it is, and in Donald and myself, not the down-at-heel laird and retainer they had imagined at our first encounter, but like them-selves simply two transient denizens of the hills.

"There's only one thing," I said; " there's a fireplace here, as you see. Now if we only had some wood, what a difference it would make to this damp and chilly place... Think how glorious it would be to have a fire." Cambridge reckoned there was something in what I said, and raised the question if there was any wood handy around. "Bynack sheiling is only a mile from here," I said; "and it would be nothing for two fit characters like you to nip across there; and if you did, we could get all the wood we want." I had not over-estimated the energy and enthusiasm of our visitors. They were on their feet in an instant, seizing the piece of rope I offered them for bundling up the wood. "You're grub will be ready for you when you get back," I said as a final inducement, if any was required.

The door screeched, and they were gone. Darkness held no terrors for this intrepid pair, and in any case they had already tumbled on Bynack sheiling on the last stage of their journey to Lower Geldie Lodge. The candle wavered in the draught of their departure, an exotic fragrance from the billy on the primus announced that the second brew was ready, and Donald and I were left alone in a bare, gloomy room still redolent, as it seemed to me, of the personality of Bob McLean, as I had last been with him there. Donald, in his slow, deliberate way, was rummaging in his rucksack for tins of stew. Then he suddenly seemed to grasp the magnitude of our fellow sojourners' sacrifice of self in the interests of the community. "Sydney," he said; "These are two really good chaps."

While Cambridge, young, indomitable and inexhaustible, was away over the Bynack getting wood, Donald and I got on with drinking our tea, cooking the dinner, and having a desultory blether about previous adventures of ours in the hills. These were not many, since this was only the second trip I had been on with my cousin, but they included a very friendly contretemps the previous September with the Braemar bobby, the very same enforcer of law and order in that area who told Bob and me on our descent from the Lairig where the best place was to poach a salmon in the Dee.

The notion of Birnam wood walking to Dunsinane seemed so absurd to Macbeth that he reckoned that he was safe in his usurpation of Scotland if that was all he had to be afraid of. The notion of Bynack wood walking to Lower Geldie Lodge might have seemed absurd to Donald and me, had not we presently beheld it with our own eyes, for the door screeched open to admit two Cambridge undergraduates so laden with combustibles that it was hard to recognise them as human beings, and not some strange creatures fashioned by the hamadryads of Bynack sheiling out of odd windfall and deadfall. The building shook as this lot was chucked on the floor, and•when the darkness had been shut out where it belonged, the grub dispatched, and the fire got going, we sat round it, the four of us, warming our knees of our breeks and drinking our tea. Socks steamed on strings, the next brew, already sizzling, hung on the hook and chain which dangled down the chimney, and the flaring larch-branches peppered the surrounding hearth with a fusillade of sparks. Donald puffed his Falcon briar meditatively, the luxury sinking into his soul which is associated with any bothy fire.

If I had my way, Hadrian's Wall would be rebuilt, manned night and day, and orders given that no tourists be allowed into Scotland. The move to prostitute the beauty of Scotland to this trade in my opinion is the last and most ignominious phase in the history of our decline and fall. At this stage a country becomes a mere corpse infested with maggots, though in this case it is those maggots that are keeping the corpse going. It is a bad state of affairs when Scotland is kept in a state of suspended animation by English and American money. The English invasions of the 13th and 14th centuries were preferable to this. They left nothing standing but at least they gave birth to a rebirth of democracy which, starting with stricken Scotland, spread across Europe and the world. Non propter gloriam aut divitias aut honoras pugnamus sed propter liberatum solum mode quan nemo bonus nisi cum vita amittit - we fight not for glory nor riches nor honours but for liberty alone which no good man lays down but with his life. They gave rise to one of the most popular expressions of the notion of liberty in any language in any part of the world:

> "Ah freedom is a noble thing
> Freedom mays man to haf liking,
> Freedom all solace to man gives,
> He lives at ease that freely lives."

Out of the burning fields, the smoking steadings and the piled corpses of the Scottish country folk came something good, if only that the identity of a people came forged from the flames of tyranny and butchery. What is likely to be the outcome of these modern invasions which we call tourist trade ? Be sure that it will be nothing good as the Scots become agents in the financial exploitation of their land.

Mind you, if a Hadrian's Wall were built to protect the last remnants of the honour of Scotland, a few chinks would have to be left here and there for visitors we would gladly welcome. I cannot be bothered working out the permitted categories of these, but they would certainly include climbers and hill-walkers, especially as many of that number as brought to these activities a reflective, philosophical and poetic turn of mind. For these are the sort of people who enrich their own country and honour any other presence. No prohibition at the border, for instance, however stringent, would have been anything other than misapplied had it not admitted the two Englishmen who now shared with Donald and me the fire that now roared up the lum at Lower Geldie Lodge, indulging ourselves in a succession of black brews of tea, and the contents of a quarter bottle of White Label produced from the depths of my rucksack.

Whether in thumbed car, train, dentist's waiting room or hill bothy, these were two of the nicest fellows you could ever hope to meet. I say two Englishmen, and certainly the name Titball seems to take us right back to the days when Harold got an arrow in his eye. Milne, on the other hand betrays a Scottish origin somewhere, so where as Roger, with husky, incisive voice was of unalloyed English pedigree, the quiet-spoken David who was an example of one of those terrible ethnic tragedies whereby someone in the ordinary run of events should have been born and brought up in Scotland gets his upbringing and education in England instead.

Such unfortunates not only carry the stigma of these early influences to the grave, but also in some cases are haunted by bitterness at their loss. Some of these become the most passionate and vituperative Scottish nationalists, flaunting the kilt and wearing daggers down their stocking, but at the same time, for all their painstaking efforts, unable to conceal their English accent. Others, like a pal of mine, Jack Cook, never forgive their father and mother for causing them to be born in England, and go to their graves muttering imprecations at the country of their forced adoption.

How recently the Englishness had crept into his family, I did not find out, but this David Milne seemed to betray none of the symptoms of the dislocated Scot. There was not one jot or tittle of flagrant Caledonianism about his apparel; and, however many generations back, he failed to mutter with a sigh the name of any ancestor as the first to repudiate the country of his origin in favour of residence in the south. Nevertheless, while Titball had all that congenital self-confidence of the Englishman which is in such blatant contra-distinction to the inferiority complex of the Scot, there was just a hint in Milne of that shyness and uncertainty which under-lies the Scottish character, even when it is expressing itself in rampant aggression.

At any rate, we chatted away the evening together in variegated causerie, philo-sophical, literary, geographical and anecdotal, in the course of which I made the two undergraduates smile by recalling a bon mot relating to their alma mater which I originally got from Reg Winnington-Ingram, Professor of Greek at London Univer-sity, and at the time, smiling complacently at his having at last finished his edition of "Bacche". "At Cambridge," so ran the mot "you dons work too hard. Here at Oxford we educate by our mere presence."

The fire had subsided into a glowing ash, the empty quarter-bottle placed on the sagging mantleshelf as an inspiration to subsequent sojourners, time to doss down, Donald and I in our chosen spot, and Roger and David shut behind doors in the mysteries of the hay filled box-bed. Silence reigned outside as it had done when McLean and I were here the year before, and as it had done twenty two years earlier when I was with Colin Brand, and in all likelihood did during the millenia when there wasn't even a Scotland as such to worry people whether they belonged to it or not, a darkness and silence at one with the primaeval order of things.

How strange, if we could wake up and see, by some dislocation of time the land-scape as it used to be, a forest of Caledonian pines stretching in every direction, and the crashing through windfall of a wild auroch as I once heard moose in the Cana-dian Rockies. How much stranger still to see in speeded up film of the transition through climatic change and human settlement from stone-age pre-Pict, to Pict and savage Scot, clan fighting clan, lifting each others' cattle and droving them. Then the carving up of the clan-lands, the sell-out for sport, and the first pomaded Victo-rian in knickerbockers whoever he was to whom this was deer forest, high lonely country where he would build lodges and bothies...... Such were my thoughts as I was drowsing off in some kind of a dwam far removed from the present.

I was thinking too of people you meet, and after a brief encounter never see each other again. I can think of hundreds of such encounters, transient, yet so many of these people were on the same wave-length as myself that it was as if I had always known them and always would. The encounters could be so perfect, so that any follow up could not improve but only diminish the original encounter. It is almost as if, where such encounters are concerned, you would go out of your way to avoid a repetition, knowing the impossibility that you should ever, as Mr Browning put it, recapture the first careless rapture. These are momentary friendships in which you do not have to undergo the trials inherent in the Johnsonian prescription that you have to keep them under constant repair. Few things, again, improve by repetition. There is nothing like the first time you heard the Chaconne for unaccompanied violin by Bach, or saw the Capitoline Venus with your own eyes, gazed down into the Garbh Choire from high perched eyrie on Braeriach, or even put a match to your pipe in the morning. Correspondingly, this encounter of mine with Roger Titball and David Milne, perfect as it was after its kind, was never either to be dulled or so much as reintegrated by repetition.

When we shook hands the next morning, themselves to move away in the direction of Lochnagar, Donald and myself to drift down the Tilt, it was never to meet again, at least in the twelve years between then and now. We did not leave Lower Geldie Lodge, however, before a little barney had occurred to mar the idyllic detachment of life in places such as these. We were by no means up with the lark the next morning, in so far as larks still sing at that time of year at that altitude, but paid for our late night blether, as you always do, by missing an hour or two which otherwise you might have enjoyed in the morning.

You cannot burn the bothy candle at both ends; and it was due, therefore, to an unavoidable sluggardliness that we had barely got up in the morning, Donald and myself from our bags on the floor, and the expatriate Cambridge men from the inscrutability of their box-bed, when the local deerstalker burst in, to sweep the interior scene with a dark and suspicious gaze. There is something which happens to deerstalkers during the shooting season whereby they are inclined to change from the easy, pleasant fellows you have become accustomed to during the rest of the year, and become distant and unpredictable, almost as if the rut which has set in amongst the stags communicates itself to them in some sublimated and mysterious form.

On the other hand, it is probably just an instance of what in biology or zoology is called "the peck order" manifesting itself when, in August, the laird suddenly appears on the scene and starts chivvying the stalkers, who all the rest of the year are accustomed to getting along without suffering his kingly presence. They get along with culling the hinds, keeping down the foxes and reading their "People's Journal" without being bothered, as it were, by the insolence of office. Being pecked themselves, the stalkers look round for somebody else to peck further down the scale, and for this retaliatory process the odd walker or climber may come in handy, since otherwise the stalker may find himself in the frustrated position of having no one at all upon whose head to relieve his injured susceptibilities.

At any rate, the stalker on this occasion, having swept the room in vain for evidence of bad tenancy on our part, ripped-up floorboards, broken window-panes and the like, suddenly spotted the box-bed, crammed voluptuously with hay as it was for the accommodation of our bagless friends. Now this hay had been taken the previous night from a store of the same piled in the porch of the Lodge, and in this misappropriation, as he saw it, of his pony fodder for base human use, the stalker, a burly man in tweeds, saw an opportunity of visiting upon inferior beings whatever pecks he had been recently subjected to by a laird, fractious and irritable with the cares of his vast estate. He snapped out as far as I remember: "We allow people like you to stay in these places, and look how you repay us for our indulgence !"

I am not a great believer in antagonising authority. We could have told him to go and eat coke, or added with a touch of menace, since we were four and he was one, that we didn't like his tone, but a policy of conciliation usually pays in the end. You scratch the stalker's back and some where, some day, he may scratch yours. It was in this persuasion I made a show of apology, assuring the stalker we had used his hay only because it was a matter of life or death for our friends, and that having used it, we had every intention of putting it back, so that the ponies would never know it had been disturbed.

That hard man Bob McLean misinterprets this inordinate friendliness of mine at best being due to apprehension and weakness of character, and at worst to a lickspittle vein of sycophancy in me; but I think he is wrong on both counts. True, I have as strong an instinct of self preservation in me as the next man, and if I thought craven submissions would serve the interest of this I would be prepared to use it, and McLean could bluster and argue with the deerstalker as much as he liked, equally persuaded that it was in his best interests to behave this way.

Each of these reactions, however, are equally removed from the mean of amiable acception of reproof which I now evinced in this petty contretemps in Lower Geldie Lodge, and which was, in my opinion, not only the best thing then but also in all such cases.

It did the stalker good to get rid of his spleen; it did me no harm to acknowledge the fault: so between us we licked the moral and emotional platter clean. The stalker was only kicking the cat, and on the understanding of this I was perfectly happy to oblige him. He was mollified by a combination of meekness, good humour and inoffensive imperturbability. Aggression would have incurred his enmity, a fawning submission mere increase of high-handedness. As it was, he had readjusted his soul without causing me in any way to maladjust mine.

"See that you put that hay back," he growled, disappearing thereafter in the pursuit of his lonely vacation.

CHAPTER ELEVEN

In June, 1961, via the Red Bothy, which is under Carn nan Gabhar of the Glen Fearnach side, Gavin and I arrived by way of Glen Tilt in late afternoon at Bynack sheiling. We had none of the usual impedimenta associated with the hills. Rucksacks, sleeping-bags, stove and all that modern rubbish had been left at home in the interests of an exercise, as we thought of it designed to give us some idea of what it might have been like to be a fugitive from Culloden. Only in imagination were Cumberland's dragoons at our heels, but for the rest we had kilts on, cape-groundsheets to sleep in, and hung about ourselves were such things as billy cans, salt, bags of oatmeal, a few tins of bully beef, a quantity of whisky, and an Army machete borrowed from Leslie Bowman for chopping up wood for fires.

By no means really bad, the weather was bleak, grey and windy, with never a blink of sun all day to symbolize with its cheerful gleam the least promise for the Jacobite cause, the collapse of which in battle still rang in our ears, as we toiled up the Allt Garbh Buidhe, passed the remains of the summer sheilings, then dropped down the bouldery track to the Bynack in its little stand of larch. Beinn Bhrotain loomed ahead of us gloomy as usual, Beinn-y-Ghlo lay far in our rear, and somewhere over the hill, with its meandering river, rock-girt pools and flat, green haughs, was a distant Glen Ey, the objective of our next day's journey.

After a night in the Altanour Lodge there, our way would be by the White Stone Burn, under Ben Iutharn Mhor, the Glen Mhor burn, The Fealar basin, and so to Jim McIntyre's cottage at the Daldhu and the termination, we trusted, of four heroic days in the hills. I tagged along behind Gavin's kilted person on the boggy approaches to the Bynack. He wore old army boots cut down into shoes. The old saying, "You canna tak' the breeks aff a Hielanman," raises the question of which is the better garment for the hills. It is a question which never arose in the old days, since in the first place the savage clansmen, whoever they were, who led their nasty, brutish lives in purlieus of the Lairig Ghru did not wear the kilt as we know it. This is a French garment which made its appearance late on the scene. The Highlander of old would have scratched his head in perplexity faced with the problems of setting and sewing all these fancy pleats. It was the tailors of Paris, I suspect, somewhere in the 16th century who answered this problem when they rigged out a few expatriate noblemen in the present fashion. The kilt as we know it gradually filtered its way down to the humbler members of clan society.

Finally Queen Victoria, waving her sceptre over the Balmoral scene, arranged things, following the lead given by Sir Walter Scott, so that all sorts of people suddenly blazed forth in the kilt. The practical dress of native Highlanders was not the dandified garment we see at the Perth Hunt Ball, but a kind of shapeless dressing gown of coarse woollen cloth known as the philibeg mhor, a garment capable of being kilted up at the knee for wading burns, charging an enemy or sleeping in, a dress that was also a blanket. The tailors of France cut the philibeg mhor in two, so as to convert it into a sophisticated plaid, for the upper part of the body and kilt for the lower part. In second place, neither the kilt or the philibeg mhor is much use as a walking garment. Breeks are best for the hills. The kilt is all right for a day on low ground in nice summer weather. In winter, if you intend going high it is better left hanging in the wardrobe. As for the legend of its utility in war, this was dispelled once and for all by the experience of the Highland regiments at Loos and the Somme. Lice were the only benefactors from its use in the trenches.

When you are trying to get to sleep and there aren't really enough covers to keep you warm, there is a position somewhere of maximum self insulation, which if you can get your body composed into it, will make it just possible to be warm enough to enable you to get over, even if you are doomed to wake up in the end half frozen to death. Alasdair Haggart, at one time Provost of St. Paul's Episcopal cathedral in Dundee, got benighted once in the glen, lay down in the lee of a dry stane dyke, and by dint of finding this self-insulating position I have just spoken of, fell asleep. When he awoke, he was so stiff with the cold that it took him half an hour of crawling round on hands and knees before he was thawed enough to stand up. Nothing like this was likely to happen in Bynack sheiling in the month of June, but nevertheless, what with a gey chilly atmosphere and the want of a good, thick pair of climbing breeks, it was not easy to get over, and as I wriggled around trying to get myself into a cosy ball, I could hear Gavin chopping away outside, so that he sounded like the final dramatic scene in Chekov's "The Cherry Orchard."

This turned my mind to the plight of the decadent Russian aristocracy in the era preceding the revolution, as also to sinister points of comparison between those times in Russia and the age in which it was the fate of my generation to grow up. From here by some twist in the labyrinth of association, I got back to the Highlanders of old, and in particular recollected the practice attributed to them of dipping their plaids in the burn before wrapping themselves up in them preparatory to a night in the open. Whether this kept the campaigning Highlander any warmer is a question we would have to put to the physicists, unless Gavin and I were prepared to set up here and now an experiment on our own account. Certainly, woollen fabric, when wet would keep the wind out better; but then, would not the heat thus retained be lost in its turn by the evaporation of the wetness ?

Colin Brand must have read his "Legend of Montrose" before me, because this matter of the wetted plaids was new to me when he mentioned it twenty three years previously in this same Bynack sheiling; as also the treatment meted out to Highlanders in the army of Montrose who piled up snow to form a pillow. "Other Highlanders kicked these pillows away," Colin informed me, "and jeered at them for being softies."

I was awakened by Gavin's step on the bare boards, and his voice quietly exultant with success. "I've got a fire going upstairs, Sydney," he said; "and you could roast a wee ox on it." For some reason Gavin had chosen the bedroom hallowed for me with memories of fires there with such people as Colin Brand and the Count of Maryfield, when we had made our way cautiously up the smashed staircase ..... almost moderately difficult now in rock-climbing terms .... and sat down on a shoogly log provided by some past sojourners, I spoke to Gavin about these ancient cronies of mine in these parts as we got on with the business of having our grub.

"Colin," I said, munching bully beef and drinking tea the while; "was always a chap of infinite resource, and this was shown by something he did after the war quite as much as anything he did in the hills before it." For the ex-clerk of Adam Will the builder, bent over his lowly ledgers, having worked his way up to a captain of signals during the War, returned to civvy street to perform what I have always thought of as a remarkable feat of ingenuity, drive and imagination.

"It was well seen, Gavin," I said, " that Colin had gifts when a decadent civilization pounced upon its efforts to destroy itself, yet pointedly ignored when those same gifts might have been used in its maintenance and regeneration." Colin, married now with a family, got a job with a firm at Springfield, Cupar, which went in for pre-cast concrete, and it was not very long till grumbles broke out among the staff about the prospects for them all in a pretty ramshackle concern. One morning when they were having their morning cup of tea, always a vital time in the affairs of British industry, Colin put a proposition to them. "I've got an idea of starting up on my own, if any of you want to join me ?" As well as brains and vision Colin had always exuded some kind of magic. An ex-Major of the Royal Engineers was first to volunteer. "I don't know what you've got in mind, but I'm willing to take a chance on it." Gavin adjusted the fire "What happened then ?"

In my mind's eye, I could see Colin sitting where Gavin sat now, the dark hair and visionary, grey eyes; only it was in a room considerably less dilapidated, less in its death throes than it was now. Gavin was in the embryo stage, as Colin had been in those days. "The bold Colin got himself admitted to the manager's office in the paper mill at Guardbridge, pointed dramatically out of the window at a towering bing of old clinker from the furnaces, and asked if he could have the use of it for his purposes." The fire began to scorch my bare knees, but with a bitter draught playing on the back of my neck, I went on to tell Gavin how the manager of the mill got interested in Colin's idea when he explained it, even offering to lay on electricity to give Colin a start.

Building materials were scarce after the War, a vast national housing program was under way, and it was Colin's intention, with the assistance of cement, much hard work, and his Major pal, to convert that bing of an old clinker into briese blocks which could not only be used in the rehousing of the Scottish masses, but get him an independent living as well. Colin's capital equipment was very simple, and in fact cost him ten shillings, an old concrete mixer with a sapling growing up through it, which he noticed in a field. Using this and wooden moulds, he and the Major knocked up, the first briese blocks were made, and out of these the two of them built a shed standing in the lee of the bing.

"When you wanted your tea," Colin told me; "you just stuck your billy somewhere in the bing itself, and there was enough heat to boil your water for you." Thereafter, they turned out briese blocks between them till there was such a pile of them that it dwarfed the shed and bade fair, if they remorselessly carried on, to equal the bing in size. The only trouble was that nobody was buying the briese blocks, so that eventually the Major's nerve broke, he quitted the concern and Colin was left alone with his bing, his shed and his briese blocks, wondering what the next move was.

"What did he do at this stage, Sydney," said Gavin: "shoot himself with his old Army revolver ?" I told him that far from that, Colin took on a Pole, convinced him that his enterprise was destined to be economically viable in the end, whatever the late Major thought of it. Working with the blind ferocity of the Slav, this Pole so increased Colin's production that if the first lorries had not presently arrived from customers to diminish its size, the pile of briese blocks might have got to the stage where it would have had to be taken account of by the Ordnance Survey.

"I was beginning to think in terms," said Colin to me; "of a trig point on top." This was the turn of the tide. Colin's brother-in-law, Irvine Rae, joined him in the enterprise, and the process began of Colin paying off his overdraught at the bank. "What happened in the end," said Gavin, obviously looking for some dramatic climax to this stirring saga of industry, or, as it might be, exercising a gentle touch of raillery: "did they all perish in an avalanche of briese blocks ?" Refreshed by my nap, warmed by the fire, and adequately nourished with bully beef and brose, I passed over the Dewar's to my fellow Jacobite. "No," I had to admit, regretful at having to disappoint him: "But what they did do is finish up buying the pre-cast concrete factory in Springfield from which Colin had set forth in the beginning."

A bleak wind shook the ruins of Bynack sheiling from time to time, the draught fairly buffeted us through the vacant, dilapidated window, and our shadows, cast by the fire, wavered on the wall in eerie chiaroscuro. Anguish, as I said before somewhere, is a prerequisite of joy; and by the same token, comfort is only to be experienced in the relaxation of discomfort, and the greater the discomfort, the smaller the relaxation needs to be. Luxury is therefore a relative term, so that it could be experienced perhaps in a greater intensity in a Japanese P.O.W. camp than in the penthouse of a Manhattan millionaire. Gavin and I had had a long day and, I suppose, a hardish one, exercise "Culloden" had imposed upon our arrangements a more stringent austerity than usual in hills, and now this fire, which blazed so cheerily up the lum and warmed us through and through, converted this house which the Dundee Sanitary would have condemned out of hand, into a palace beside which Versailles in all its glory shrank to the status of a hovel. Sin was invented by the first man to be sinless, namely Jesus; stink was invented by the first man to wash: and Gavin and I were re-discovering the fact that comfort first burst upon the world, not in the banqueting chamber of Lucullus, the baths at Pompeii, or the sinister villa of Tiberius on Capri, but in the squalor of places like Bynack sheiling.

Old Mr McKenzie, ex-Police Sergeant at Kingussie and father-in-law of Louis the post, was wont to say that a kilt was not really in a fit state to wear till it was getting ragged at the edge; and certainly my kilt, a hunting Stewart, was well advanced in this class. My claim to wear this tartan, if it could be upheld as a claim at all under Highland rules and regulations regarding dress, rested in the fact that my maternal grandmother's mother-in-law, who came from Kinlochrannoch and had the Gaelic, was called Kirstie Stewart, and a crabbit auld bitch she was, according to my Aunt Annie Bewick, whom was just old enough to have picked up a few words of the Gaelic from this Highland déracinée, then in extreme old age living in St. Peter Street, Dundee.

My kilt must always be a melancholy reminder, not only of the failure of the House of Stewart at Culloden in whose service Gavin and I were now, at least in imagination, but also of the shocking end of this Kirstie Stewart: "For," I told Gavin, "beshawled and clad in lace mutch, and with a candle glimmering by her side, she used to read her bible every night in bed, presumably as a preparation against never waking up again. One night, the candle set fire to her mutch and that was the end of old Kirstie."

It is hard to be reverential at such a remove of time, and Gavin observed smiling, that in inexperienced hands the Bible is a pretty dangerous book even at the best of times, as evidenced by the fratricidal conflicts, even up to the present, of the various Christian denominations whose apparently incompatible zeals derive from a study of the self same scriptures. "That book has done more harm, as well as more good," he said "than anything else that ever rolled off the printing presses of the world."

For his part my learned young friend had a Cameron kilt, and Gavin proceeded to give me a short lecture on the branch of that clan from which he himself was descended. Squeezed out, apparently, by social pressures from their indigenous Lochaber, a tatterdemalion band of this clan settled in Fife at a place known to this day as Cameron Brig, so that they now have the distinction, if no other, of having the only brand of pure grain Scots whisky called after them. It was through his maternal grandmother that Gavin laid claim to his tartan, a woman so stiffly critical of the decadence with which she found herself latterly surrounded, that it is with the word "preposterous" on her lips that her surviving relatives chiefly recollect her.

It was not with memories embodied in bloody affray, cattle rieving and odd massacres here and there that Gavin and I now sat in our kilts in Bynack sheiling, but with familia trivia come down to us from our elders. It was time for us to move on to Lower Geldie Lodge, a doss that Gavin was keen to hansel, so we left the grey slatted Bynack, the grass-covered blocks of its old steading, and its nodding larches, crossed the footbridge which sagged over the Bynack burn, and holding to the high ground which divides the two waters, dropped down on the Geldie bridge, the surrounding hills meantime watching us as if suspicious of what was going on.

An eeriness in the hills which furtively skulks in the concealment of the corries by day, seems to spread out in the gloaming enlarging to embrace the whole landscape. No troll reached out of the ground, however, to seize a passing ankle; no kelpie stuck its hideous face out of a glimmering pool: nor did we hear the phantom thudding of hoofs and clinking of spur, and recognize in vague, grey shapes any echo, as it were of those dragons of old who pursued and mercilessly cut down the fleeing Jacobite prototypes of ourselves. "On the whole," said Gavin, «as he pushed open the screeching door of Lower Geldie Lodge; "I'm glad this is not the real thing."

Some where in the opening chapters of "Moby Dick" and with reference to Ishmael and Queequweg, who are sharing a bed in a lodging together, Herman Melville dwells on what a wonderful arena the bed is for cosy and intimate chats. Perhaps it is the warmth that has something to do with it, for it is hard to open your heart to someone when you are shivering with cold under a boulder at the Allt Choire Mhoir; perhaps it is the darkness, which provides conditions analogous to those of the psychiatrist's couch: but at any rate, bed can be a kind of amiable confessional in which two chaps will divulge to each other without embarrassment the innermost secrets of their souls.

I do not assert that the hills have any special advantage in this respect, but it is sunk in sleeping-bags in such places as Luibeg, Corrour bothy and the Sinclair hut, as much as anywhere else, that I have heard the words: "I have never told this to a soul before." Nothing of this reciprocal imparting of private experience, so far as I can remember, occurred between Gavin and I in our box-bed in Lower Geldie Lodge, though what with the hay inside and the two doors you can shut, a box-bed is perfectly adapted to this kind of thing.

But we were reasonably warm there, which we would not have been at the Bynack as soon as the fire died down, and as we huddled together, head to feet in the darkness and confinement, I passed on to Gavin a story brought to my mind by the coldness at the knees I had experienced at the Bynack earlier that evening. It is possible Gavin fell asleep in the middle, for there was not so much as a sleepy grunt of acknowledgement at the end.

Some where on the upper Arno, it was reported to us by Regimental Intelligence, and in a castle which commanded the glen from a high plug of rock, it was the daily practice of the opposing Germans to plant an O.P. by means of which our positions were blasted from time to time with pretty accurate shell and mortar fire. It was a small consolation to us learning that this was one of the castles where Dante Alighieri, the Italian poet, writer of the "Divine Comedy", took refuge in his period of exile from Florence. There was nothing divine about the comedy we found ourselves in. Somebody had the idea of laying an ambush for these Germans, to discourage them from thinking they could use this castle as an Observation Post to direct destroying fire on us.

They were to be reminded, these grey-clad minions of Marshall Kesselring that Clauswitz was not to be permitted always to have his own way. The Lovat Scouts could bring to bear on this tactical problem some of the know-how gained not only at G.H.Q. Battle School, County Durham, but also on a hundred Highland deer forests and grouse moors. Accordingly, I was sent forward with some of the boys, and it was while snatching an hour's sleep in the F.D.L.'s prior to working our way into the disputed terrain ahead that cold knees occurred, the recent counterpart of which called this little operation to mind. "We woke up," I told Gavin in the confines of our box-bed, "fairly shaking with cold." It was still dark when the ambush was set up at the most likely spot; and when dawn broke, followed by the sunrise of yet another glorious Tuscan day, and no Germans appeared, no one could have been more pleased than one small, apprehensive detachment of Lovat Scouts. Shooting is the last thing any soldier wants to get involved in. He is all for the peaceful life as long as this is consistent with the triumph of his cause, and it was therefore in a very happy frame of mind that I decided to take a look at the castle, as much for antiquarian as for military reasons. "Wait here," I said to "Picket" McDonald. He was my corporal, a Torridon man, and a very good chap he was: "I'll come back in a wee while." Time passed, the sun rose higher and higher in the sky, and when his commander was never reappearing, "Picket" began to wonder if something had gone wrong. Certainly there had been no shots, but he had visions of me being marched away into captivity by the sons of Hitler, some of whom may have been lurking all night around this Castle of Romena.

Telling the boys in his turn to stay where they were, Picket crawled forward to recce the situation. For all he knew, the whole issue of the War might turn on what lay ahead under those grey walls and in a cottage or two which were scattered around about them. If anyone could outwit Kesselring in this little contretemps, he was the man to do it, and to this end he kept a firm grasp on his tommy-gun and scanned the ground ahead like any Wester Ross stalker at the hinds.

The nearest cottage, if he could reach it unseen, seemed to present itself as a good base for further progress, so with infinite caution, Picket made his way towards it, using the ground so adeptly that the keenest-eyed German sentry, however passionately devoted to the cause of the Fuhrer, could not have suspected that there was a member of the clan McDonald in the vicinity.

Eventually Picket pulled himself up and peered in the window of the cottage. Would he see a peaceful scene of Italian domesticity, the bambino in its cradle, the mother stuffing brushwood on the fire, the padrone sitting brooding over the problems of a world at war ? Or would it be some slovenly detachment of a war-weary Reichswehr smoking their abominable fags, a Schmeisser on the table, and a Mauser rifle propped up against the wall? Picket saw neither of these things, but only his missing commander lying back in a chair in the most relaxed attitude imaginable, his hands behind his head, a look of serene complacency on his face, and his right leg resting in the lap of an Italian girl who was industriously sewing up a big tear in his breeks. The martial exploit planned for that morning, so far as this commander was concerned, had obviously come to a satisfactory conclusion.

To the Linn of Dee, then, still in our role of fleeing Jacobites, Gavin and I hurried ourselves very early next morning. For one thing we were a little chilly, even after our night in the box-bed, and this emphasised the fact that we had been right in our decision to exchange a potentially chillier night at the Bynack for the comparative comfort of Lower Geldie Lodge. For another thing, there was not the ready makings of a fire where we were, no heap of kindling stacked up by the fireplace in accordance with the unwritten laws of the hill bothies; so that breakfast could only have consisted of oatmeal and salt stirred up with cold water, a "dramach" which the mind shrunk from in that bleak apartment, when the fingers were a little numb and the blood sluggish in the veins.

That kind of thing might have been good enough for the authentic Jacobites under the weight of catastrophic defeat, but we were in the happier position of being able to fluctuate at will between fantasy and reality, and Gavin had a much more attractive prospect in mind once we got down to the Linn five miles away. He knew that the Boys Brigade were there in all the comfortable reassurance of bell tent and marquee, and through the good offices of a pal of his, David Husband, an officer in the B.B. company in question, he knew we would be entertained to breakfast should no unforeseeable disaster overtake us between here and the Linn. Our footsteps, therefore, only echoed in the emptiness of the Lodge for a short time that morning. Then the door screeched: the Geldie swirled along away down on the right, the higher Cairngorms loomed on the left, somewhat menacing in the grey morning light, and

Ruigh nan Clach, standing back a bit from the road as it does, gazed at us mournfully as we crunched past, as if to say, why do these fellows always spend their nights at Lower Geldie Lodge and never here. "Clach" means a boulder and "ruigh" a greenmeadow or haugh; and sure enough in its immediate surroundings this now empty building satisfies the requirements laid down for it by its name.

Here and there in all this locality are the "larachs" which are indicative of past settlement, the mere ground-plan of old fanks and dwellings, now overgrown with grass or heather. The occupants of this region were no doubt evicted in consequence of that glaring crime against humanity usually referred to by the pleasant euphemism of the "clearances", so that where there was once life and society of some kind, there is now desolation.

> "When the bold kindred in the time long
> vanished
> Conquered the soil and fortified the
> keep,
> No seer foretold the children would be
> banished
> That a degenerate lord might boast his
> sheep."

From where the River Dee originates in those brisk wells amongst the boulders, moss and grit of Braeriach, to where it feels the rise and fall of the salt sea in the vicinity of the stinking fish-markets of Aberdeen, there is no part of its course more spectacular, than where the river, pretty broad as it sweeps past White Bridge, suddenly narrows between jutting rock ledges at the Linn, and hurls itself in a jet of swirling foam into the pool below. There is an old, blotched notice in the vicinity, perhaps for the benefit of leaping salmon as well, reminding passers-by of the difference between young salmon and salmon parr; pines stand around, whose rustle is lost in the roar of the waters: and a stone bridge carries the Braemar road past Linn cottage both to the gate where the Tilt track starts and to the Derry gate beyond, where civilization begins to totter at the ultimate outset to the Lairig Ghru.

This bridge and the racing cataract below apparently fascinated Edwards, the great Welsh rock-climber, as he passed by that way, a rucksack on his back and his mind filled, no doubt, with the prospects of fresh discoveries in the high Cairngorms.

He had, this brooding Welshman, just that touch of craziness which in rock-climbing separates genius from mediocrity, and as he gazed at the boiling waters below him, there stirred in his mind an idea which sanity would have immediately rejected, but which the madness of this solitary figure eagerly embraced. With Edwards, to think was to act. After all he had hurled himself up overhangs on Tryfan and Grib Goch without the slightest knowledge of whether there were handholds up there or not; and now he unslung his rucksack, placed it on the ground, stripped himself off to his underpants, vaulted on to the parapet of the bridge, and dived headfirst into the maelstrom below.

The thing was done so quickly that a few odd bystanders had no time to intervene in what must be some new form of suicide. All these rock-climbing chaps had a death-wish. Was it because he had consistently failed to fulfil this on his native crags, wherever these were, that this poor chap had now been driven to the expedient of which they were the appalled witnesses? One moment he poised there, the next he was gone and when they rushed towards the parapet, it was to see, already three hundred yards away, a dark head appearing and disappearing in the foam, and arms which cleft the water as it raced the doomed man along. It took them a good while these assorted observers, to get over their shock.

In war, another dead man here and there is a matter of no concern. The Imperial War Graves Commission will attend to him in the end and that is all. In peace the spectacle of a life wantonly thrown away is inclined to fill the beholder with solemn thoughts regarding the transient brevity of all human existence. Boots, rucksack and a pile of assorted hill garments; these were now all that remained of what had only a moment ago been a human life with all its potential for good or evil, tragic symbols of a unique concatenation of chemicals, now for ever passed away.

Presently, however a figure was descried trudging along the road towards them and in an instant they recognised in that bare chest and underpants, now soggy with water, the chap they had unhesitatingly written off as dead, and whose belongings still stood there to prove it. Silently they parted to let him through. There were no words, it seemed to them, adequate to the occasion. Edwards donned his clothes, heaved his rucksack up on his shoulders, cast what seemed to the observers a somewhat contemptuous glance at the frenzied Dee below, then resumed his brooding progress towards the Derry gate. The pines swallowed him up, and with his disappearance, a wave of blessed normality swept back over the world.

Gavin was no stranger to the Linn of Dee, and as a child had greatly excited his parents by getting too close to the edge and nearly falling in. I told him about the chap that fell in here, a doctor on his honeymoon, his wife able to do nothing but watch. They managed to pull him out, alive. His wife fainted with relief, fell in and got drowned. Gavin had not heard of this horrifying event, an event which almost seemed to point to some malignant entity at the Linn, which cheated of one prey, made haste to snatch another while the time was ripe.

As we trudged down the road he enlarged on this malignancy where the Dee thunders between narrow rock walls. He had rushed down with his brother and sister to look over at the swirling cataracts, failed to spot the slipperiness of the shelving rocks, lost his footing, teetered on the brink, and would have gone over the edge if his sister Catherine had not stuck out her hand. He pulled her down but Ian the eldest of the three got a hold on his sister and saved the other two.

They hadn't been seen by anyone, so immediately there was a pledge of secrecy to tell nothing of what happened. So their parents never knew that it was by the merest fluke that the Sprott family returned to Braemar in the same numerical strength as they had departed earlier that day.

The B.B. camp on its green haugh, close to the rippling waters of a broader Dee, the welkin ringing with the cries of a junior Dundee was just the place to dispel the eerie gloom of the Linn, and we were ready for all there was in the way of porridge and milk, kippers, big slices of bread and mugs of hot, sweet tea in the clamorous and hospitable marquee.

Being so near the fleshpots, it was more than two travel-stained Jacobites could do, to resist the temptations of Braemar, we had run out of provisions, meagre as these were, and in particular a further bottle of Dewar's to see us via Altanour Lodge to our ultimate destination at Daldhu in Glen Fearnach. "If this whisky was good enough for my grandfather," I said alluding to that charming, if drunken, old reprobate Peter Bewick, who in his day travelled far for the firm in question, "Then it's good enough for me."

To an older generation the village of Inverey near the Linn of Dee is forever associated with the Cairngorms, for in Thistle Cottage there lived a Deeside worthy by the name of Maggie Gruer who knew and made welcome every hill man and woman given to stravaiging the Lairig Ghru in the 20's and 30's.

A fleet of cars bearing Cairngorm Club members would arrive to first foot Maggie at New Year. Her Chair was given to the President of that most senior of Scottish climbing clubs on her death, and becomes the presidential seat at the annual club dinner. Her mother began the tradition of hospitality to walkers. Maggie seems to have taken on the role about 1911 and continued it until her death in 1939. Her Chair and her famous Visitor's Books are treasured by the Cairngorm Club.

I never had a night at Maggie's, so have no first-hand knowledge of a woman as famous in her time as Bob Scott was in his. I have heard that Maggie liked the lads more than the lassies, to the extent that if it was a case of one or the other, the lads got the best accommodation while the lassies could make a kirk or a mill of it in the shed outside.

When I think of the village of Inverey, it is in connection with such people as Mrs McDougal, the couthy warden of the little Youth Hostel next to her cottage, and that good man Alexander Dempster, an expatriate son of Sutherland who has so often put us up in his bothy. "Bothy Closed" says a sinister notice on Alex's howff, but I have never known the day when he wouldn't open it up for you, and pass the time of day over a nip from your bottle. Old Maggie Gruer is dead but not only does her fame linger into an alien age, but also the things she stood for in the minds and souls of thousands; the hills, the glens, the smell of wood smoke on a winter morning, and that dark pass between Ben Macdhui and Braeriach. Maggie was a daughter of the croft, and these imperishable symbols will survive her forever.

Inverey is a ghost village today, a place of holiday homes, and when we were offered a lift I could not help contrasting this speedy, luxurious, little journey with an occasion twenty years ago when John Ferguson and I, soaked to the skin with our clothes freezing on as we trudged these same miles and in the same direction.

Gavin listened as patiently as usual as I embroidered the tale, cutting me short with a "What happened ? Were you toughening yourself up for the Russian front ?" I had said that Democracy had its back to the wall, also that we had a tent up the Quoich, and to save detouring to cross the Dee by Victoria Bridge at Mar Lodge had decided to ford it. He had a good reason to ask his question, for it was January, powder snow lying, and temperatures amongst the lowest I ever experienced in Scotland. At the Slugain bothy we chucked a mugful of water into the air one evening and it froze before it hit the ground. On our short-cut we first had to cross an arm of the Quoich which fingers out into a kind of delta at its confluence with the

Dee; and though this was deep, it was narrow enough to jump, but would have to be jumped without a pack. John took off his bergan and began to swing it round like a discus thrower preparatory to letting it go. As I was admiring what looked like an animated caricature of Myron's celebrated statue, I saw the bergan fly through the air, then John follow it, not of his own volition however, but because he got hooked somehow or other on the rucksack at the moment of release. There was a splash, John's bergan reappeared, bobbing gently downstream, then John himself laughing and swearing at the same time, scrambled out of the water on the far side, soaked from head to foot.

"John," I said, "if you'd practiced that for weeks you couldn't have done it better." I threw my rucksack across, then measuring the breadth of the water with my eye, decided I had better take a run at it for fear of dropping short and so giving John the opportunity for some counter sarcasm if I too fell in. Just as it is a mistake to be too casual in such matters, so apparently it is a mistake to be too cautious; and, in fact, the whole of life, I suppose, consists in striking a mean between these two extremes. Running up to the bank, I stuck my foot in a hole, to dive headfirst into that same deep, ice-fringed water from which my friend had so recently emerged. "Sydney," said John, wringing out shirt and jersey and putting them back on again; "would you like to do that again while I get a picture." Steamy enough inside, but with an exterior layer of frost-stiffened clothes, we squelched our way into a silent war-time Braemar.

Now that still winter day a thing of the past, Gavin and I got out of the car in a very different Braemar, jammed with big coaches and jostling with tourists. Dark glasses and cameras were the order of the day. A blashy shower had passed over, and the sun was hot on our cheeks. "But somewhere here still," I said to Gavin "may be the descendants of the good Braemar folk who dried John and I out."

CHAPTER TWELVE

At the end of July 1961, or a bare month after the two Jacobites in the best of spirits vanished down Glen Ey on the last stages of their imaginary flight from Culloden, I turned up at Luibeg cottage with Martin Pirie. It was a fine, sunny day with a strong wind, and already, it seemed, a legend was gaining currency around Bob's little empire that, no matter what it had been like up till then, the weather was bound to be good when the blind man from Dundee arrived. "Ay, ay, Scroggie," says Luibeg, hailing us across the open ground between cottage and bothy; "yi'v brought yir ain private weather wi' ye in yir pack, I see."

Martin was a pal of Bob McLean's, and in fact the two of them shared a flat, how, God only knows, at 36 Victoria Road, Dundee, until Bob disappeared over the horizon to grapple with his inscrutable destiny abroad, leaving a somewhat sad and thoughtful Martin behind him. "Yes," said Martin, brooding over a rum in the Victoria Bar; "I've lost the best friend I ever had." Yet there was never a more ill assorted pair shared lodging together. Martin, fussy and old-maidish, was everything that is summed up in the word "perjink" while the word "through-ither" was pretty well coined for Bob's benefit, gloriously contemptuous as he was of anything in the way of orderliness and tidiness. But the two of them got along wonderfully well, their friendship cheerfully expressing itself in a pretty well constant stream of jaunts, insults and accurately derogatory remarks. I believe this kind of thing is quite common in primitive societies, and in the case of two such incongruous room mates as Bob and Martin, in the absence of some transcendental, spiritual relationship, it was probably the only possible basis for friendship. "Ach, you McLean. You try to live here like a pig amongst shite." To which Bob would retort, laughing at the Fifer's bent brows and tart expression, "Pirie, you're naething but a crabbit auld spinster in disguise, and a gey thin disguise, too."

Bob, the journalist, encouraged Martin, the telephone engineer, to improve his reading, and one of the results of this was that this apprentice in literature found himself ploughing through "Finnegan's Wake." James Joyce, however, proved a bit too much for Martin, who was frankly mystified as to what the book was about, and a bit peeved,too, that this should be so. He suspected some kind of conspiracy on the part of a mere Dublin clerk to trip him up. "I got as far as page seven," said Martin, "and then found myself confronted with the following....

"Holy Moses, the king of the Jews
Wiped his arse with the Evening News."

....at which point I shut the book, and have never opened it again."

Bob also encouraged Martin to come to the hills with him, and it was at the outset of a trip through the Lairig from the Aviemore side that something occurred which

Bob mercilessly kept up on Martin ever afterwards. It was in May, 1959, only the week after Bob did the Lairig with me, and in the early morning coolness of the Rothiemurchus Forest, Bob got a fire going to make some tea. The fact that fires are strictly prohibited in this area would be part of the charm of the thing to Bob.

In a democratic society, these anonymous authorities that spring up everywhere like autumn mushrooms must not be suffered to promulgate their absurd fiats with impunity. If everyone started obeying grim notices like these in the Rothiemurchus Forest, we would all be slaves in no time. With thrill calls, tits and chaffinches seemed to approve this act of rebellion on the part of this wild and bearded figure, and even the old Scots pines, as it were, nodded indulgently as the first fragrance of woodsmoke wafted amongst them in the morning breeze. We would rather be burnt to the ground by this bold fellow, they seemed to be saying, than preserved by these damned Nature Conservancy people.

So Bob gets the fire going at the side of the track, hangs a billy of water over it by some ingenious tinky arrangement, lights himself a fag, and chucks the half-burnt match into the water so that it floats on the top, charred at one end, unblemished at the other. Now, as every initiate who has ever drummed up over a wood fire knows, this keeps the smoke from tasting the water, any old twig will have the same effect, the thing probably being explained by the fact that turpentine spreads outwards from the wood, so as to form a protective film against the smoke on the surface of the water. Martin did not know this, and in a sudden flare of peevishness, read in this casual act of McLean's another instance of what he deemed the insanitary habits of his friend.

Incensed beyond words, he plucked out the offending matchstick and flung it away. If things could not be done according to Atholl Crescent; this seemed to be Martin's attitude, as a chuckling McLean saw it: then, by God, it was better they were not done at all. Martin was not readily mollified when Bob, not without up-roarious taunts, explained the reason for the matchstick in the water; and as I imag-ine it, the two continued to tilt each other on this subject at least as far as the Sinky hut. "Why don't you go and live with the tinks, McLean," Martin would be saying, calculatedly vitriolic; "you might be able to drag them down to your level." Whereas Bob's voice would come floating over the bogs in amiable retort with, "Pirie, you're shaped like a man, but the spirit of Mrs Grundy or somebody like her lives on in you undaunted."

"A captain is a captain, a mate is a mate;" The Hollywood of the thirties alleges this to have been said by William Bligh, Captain of His Majesty's ship Bounty: "but a midshipman, Mr Christian, is the lowest form of life in the British Navy." In the Scottish hills, the lowest form of life is the skier, and I do not mean by this the reso-lute few who don rucksacks and planks with a view to pursuing in the winter hills those same poetical and metaphysical objectives which for some people are to be found in the hills and nowhere else.

It is hard to pursue these objectives when you are sinking up to the oxters in snow, and in keeping their wearer on the surface of the drifts between, shall we say, Cor-rour bothy and the Pools of Dee, skis are doing all that they were originally intended to do. The snow shoe was the Red Indian's solution to the problem of snow, and a reasonably effective solution so far as it goes. The wily Finn, on the other hand, devised the ski, which can do all a snow shoe can and a great deal else besides.

Under the flickering Northern Lights, the denizen of Lapland could get across the frozen wastes with much greater dexterity and flexibility on his primitive skis than ever could Sioux or Mohican, condemned to trudge cannily along on his big yeti feet of strung gut and birch spar. Faced with the same problem, that of getting around on snow, the solution of the semi-primitive Red Indian was crude and uninspired; that of the civilized Finn, sophisticated and ingenious. Just as the Red Indian of old would gaze in astonishment at the spectacle nowadays of his taboggan whizzing down the Cresta run for no other reason than to get to the bottom as quickly as possible, so the Finn of bygone times would see in idle people aimlessly whizzing down snow-slopes on his invention, all the craziness of a decadent and moribund society. Whether in Glen Coe, Glen Shee or Glen More, chair-lift and ski-tow, far from the enlightened recreational amenities their advocates make them out to be, are symptoms of mortal social disorder.

When Martin, therefore, eventually took to the ski-ing we knew that he was a doomed man and that a career in the hills which had shown much promise under the tutelage of McLean was destined to fizzle out in mere wrangling about waxes; impassioned arguments as to the comparative merits of stem and parallel christies, and the gin and tonics, soft lights, and murmurous background pop music of the apres-ski lotus life.

Now, however, it was a Martin still cast in the heroic mould designed for him by McLean, who munched scones with me by candlelight, in a bleak, because as yet fireless, Luibeg, tended the roaring primus with its precarious top load of water-filled billy can, and discussed the events of a day when we had left the Shelter Stone in the morning, climbed Macdhui by way of the rock terraces of the Garbh Uisge, descended the steep Sròn Riach, and in gathering darkness arrived at Bob Scott's lonely pied à terre in the wilderness.

The scones were a gift of Margaret, Bob's wife, and presently Luibeg himself appeared with all that energetic affability and bustling masterfulness which were always the marks of his extrovert personality. He had a new joke, and was not long in broaching it to Martin and me as the fire began to crackle in the big, granite hearth and the chill of the bothy to give way to the most genial of all warmths, that provided by a wood fire. Bob liked telling stories about the gentry, as the ghillies find them. This one was about the laird briefing his head keeper about a dark skinned maharajah. "Mind ye noo, Willy? He's a big man in his ain country so ye'll mind and gie him his title and treat him wi' proper respect." Next day, it seems, Willie observed due protocol, and was a model of patience forbye when it turned out that the maharajah was a poor hand at the fishing. "You will pardon me your Royal Highness if I jist gie ye a wee demonstration o' how to dae it correctly," he said. There was no improvement. "Na, na, na, gie's us the rod your Royal Highness an' watch mair closely this time." The maharajah was making a both of it again when the keeper snatched the rod away from him "In the name o' God, ye ignorant black nigger."

Flames leapt up the lum, the water began to tottle on the primus, and a continuing bellow of laughter as Bob made off confirmed that Bob is one of those people who, in the telling of a joke, are always their best audience. "I wonder," said Martin, measuring tea into the billy can with meticulous exactitude, "if Bob himself was the keeper in question."

Martin was busy as chef de cuisine preparing a meal, which as he placed on my lap said "What are you thinking about, Scroggie?" I had kept silent because he prefers to turn out his culinary masterpieces unimpeded by willing but incompetent assistance or the distraction of conversation. "Nothing," I replied as I got stuck into the grub with a spoon.

I'd just been listening to the crackling of the fire, the murmur of the Luibeg burn outside, a puff of wind round the bothy, and the piping of oyster catchers in the darkness. My mind had wandered to Bob Scott who was a sapper in the Royal Engineers when I was an infantry lieutenant. Whatever it cost, the War had been worth it, and in our middle years, faced with the same menace, Bob and I would shrug our shoulders, drink a last dram, and with the same mixture of eagerness and reluctance as before, march forth again. In the middle of the Lairig Ghru, utterly and totally dependent upon his friend in an alien and unknowable environment, a blind man wills his subjection to another without reservation of any kind and is wonderfully and gloriously free.

AFTERWORD AND RETROSPECTIVE

If you have been able to see, as I could, then lose your sight, you never cease to conceive of the world except in visual images. Touch a table and you see a table, smell a hyacinth and you see a hyacinth, hear a blackbird and you see a blackbird, take an orange and you see an orange; and what is true of everyday domestic things is true also of the outdoors, so that general smells, sounds and sensations of a land-scape automatically translate themselves into whatever images these stimuli suggest to your imagination.

This is also true of landscapes you have never seen, in my case where I live now. When I am on Braeriach, standing on top I recall the scene that I remember, Lochan Uaine in its hanging corrie, the scraggy slopes of Ben Macdhui, the distant glimpse of Lochnagar, vast magnificent and spacious. The same is true of Glen Clova, in all its aspects, Muick, Callater and Isla, for I knew them all by sight, whereas what is to be seen from An Teallach, Blaven, Am Bodach, Ben Vorlich, and Carn na Caim, which I never knew by sight, I can appreciate only from those who described what lay around me.

That said, I have discovered that it is not the visual side of things in the hills that constitutes the profoundest aspect of the experience, any more than it is the croak of the ptarmigan, the scent of the heather, the feel of granite under your fingers, or any other of the merely physical phenomena which are part and parcel of the hills. What draws you there is an inner experience, something psychological, something poetic, which perhaps cannot be fully understood when the physical aspect of things gets in the way when you can see.

So there is nothing paradoxical after all that a blind man should want to prowl about the hills, spend nights under the Shelter Stone, tag on behind his friends to the top of Ben Macdhui, or walk the Cairngorm Lairig, since at the deepest level, he is getting as much out of it as anyone else, especially as he has to work infinitely harder for it when one leg is wooden. I am prepared to allot only point five of one per-cent to the visual side of the hills in their power to awe and impress; the blind man is without that little amount, but the rest, and this is far more important, is as much his as to any climber, deerstalker, laird or hill shepherd. He is au fait with the heart of the matter.

My very last sight in the world was the planet Venus, bright and beautiful, pul-sating in the gloaming sky. Twenty five years of age and a Troop Leader in the Lovat Scouts, I had some of the boys out on patrol. Between us and Jerry lay the neglected vineyards and shattered farm-houses of a Romagnan landscape dominated by Monte Grande. Then an explosion, and when I came to I was sitting in a hole and leaning back on my rucksack. Inside my head, lights flashed and a red mask blocked my vision. I heard the voice of Hoppy Hoskins. "Are you all right Sir ?" he said, a hint of fear in his voice, as if he too might set off a mine like the one that had done for his Troop Leader. I have often thought subsequently how certain I was from the start what had happened to me. "I'm all right Hoppy," I said, "but I think I've lost the sight of both eyes."

The Lovat Scouts comprising many Highland deerstalkers and gamekeepers - notable sharp-shooters - joined the Allied forces in Italy after a winter in the Canadian Rockies spent in mountain commando training, and it was my good luck to get 12 Troop up Mount Columbia, which at 12,294 feet, is the second highest peak in the Canadian Rockies. It had never been climbed in winter, and on that first ascent we spent two nights in snow-holes at 9000 feet. The full moon shone. A thermometer hanging from a ski-stick registered 37° below zero. Innumerable peaks round us glittered with ice and snow.

It happened that a friend of mine, Les Bowman, fell in with some Lovat Scouts in the neighbourhood of Gratz in Austria and asked them if they knew a lieutenant called Scroggie. From them Les learned that I had got blinded, had lost the lower part of a leg and was in hospital in Naples. Les, who was serving with Popski's Private Army, an outfit noted for dash and initiative, requisitioned a jeep, loaded it with jerrycans of petrol and cases of compo-rations, and got going for Naples. He drew a blank at the first hospital, but was directed to the 92nd British up the hill. "You're a day late," they told Les, "We shipped him to the U.K. yesterday in the Atlantis."

St. Dunstan's look after war-blinded British servicemen and servicewomen, and it was there I eventually arrived, their base at that time being in the little Shropshire village of Church Stretton. Because I had a notion to go up to Oxford, there to catch up on my education, my particulars had to be taken down. This was attended to by a Cambridge don called Stanners, a tweedy, jovial bachelor, who had put himself at the service of Dunstan's where educational matters were concerned. "Where were you born?" asked Mr Stanners. My reply was "Nelson, B.C." Said Mr Stanners, "I think we'll put down British Columbia, otherwise they might think B.C. was when you were born."

Had not my father died prematurely, Lt. Col. J.A. Scroggie, D.S.O., M.C. (2 bars), Medaille Militaire, of the Canadian Permanent Force, myself and my two brothers would have grown up in the Canadians. My father, Austin Scroggie, had emigrated to Canada from Newport, Fife, in 1910, with his pal, Sydney Scott. Life was hard in the Kootenays those days, but between them the two Scots got a farm going, to have things interrupted by the outbreak of the First World War.

In Edinburgh years later I was told by Cy Peck V.C. who served with him in the War, "Your father was the best infantry officer produced by Canada." His premature death was caused by an old war wound, and my mother returned with her three little boys to Scotland, and thus it was that I found myself, at a school for fatherless children in Edinburgh, John Watson's Institution.

I was a good if careless scholar, captained the rugby side, and went down in school history as one of only two boys to have won the sports cup twice. In 1971, I was chatting to pupils there when one of them asked if I was the Sydney Scroggie who in his day put up a new record for the quarter-mile. I described the race to him, one I'll never forget, to receive the exceedingly flattering information that this record still stood.

D.C. Thomson and Co. Ltd., the Dundee publishers, took me on when I left school, made me sub-editor on the "Hotspur", and here in a fug of cigarette smoke, I had a pleasant time until the outbreak of the Second World War. This event we celebrated by making a dummy, attached to a golf umbrella, and launching it from the roof of the Courier building, spreading word around that the first German parachutist had been seen to land in the Auld Howff, Dundee's oldest and most prestigious graveyard.

It was during this period that I took to the hills, walking with Colin Brand, rock climbing with John Ferguson, found out what it was to see the dawn come up from the top of a mountain, to search for holds in some exposed and precarious situation on granite or gneiss, and in such howffs as Corrour bothy sniff the ineffable odour of paraffin, woodsmoke and sizzling bacon. Here was some kind of heaven, and few weekends saw any of us at home, few holidays anywhere other than in the Tilt, Glen Isla, Glen Fernait, or the magical recesses of the Lairig Ghru.

Glen Clova was however our spiritual home, and here we learned that it is not only the rocks, the boulders and bothies that constitute the hills, but the people who live there; the Harpers at Newbiggin, old Alan Cameron at Moulzie, these and the pals you happen to be with. But there is something which goes deeper than friendship; sense of adventure, imminence of danger, the birds, the flowers, changing patterns of light on corrie and face, something that can only be called spiritual. St. Magnus Cathedral in Orkney stands for one kind of spirituality, the Italian Chapel for another, the Standing Stones of Stenness for a third.

The founder of St. Dunstan's, Sir Arthur Pearson, said blindness should be looked upon not as a handicap but as an opportunity, and it was in this spirit I approached two opposite and equal stages of my post-war rehabilitation, Oxford and Middlebank. Five terms at New College, Oxford taught me how to read and think, sundry weekends at Middlebank, a tumble-down ruin in the country near Dundee, taught me how to saw and chop wood, scrub floors, furrow up tatties, and manage a wooden leg on rough ground.

Middlebank was where Les Bowman, demobilised from the Army, lived with his wife Betty, and he was the ideal man to have around when I was trying to get used to a new kind of life. Les acted as if I wasn't blind and had two good legs. It was a method employed by Jean Campbell, a nursing sister at a Dundee factory when her little boy got poliomyelitis. In the street, if he fell, Jean walked on, allowing him to struggle by himself, and only then would Jean lend a hand. The boy grew up without the worst thing that any disabled person can acquire, the mentality of a cripple. And if I avoided this in my own case, this was in part due to Les, as winter and summer we embarked together in various strenuous activities in the woods, fields and heather slopes around Middlebank.

The approach to the tumble-down place was by a rutted cart track a quarter of a mile off the public road. First there was a wood on your right, then a hump-backed stone bridge, a right turn followed by a left turn, and by now you were rising up a brae with a row of lime trees on your right. Down the brae you went beyond this, encountered a dilapidated dry stane dyke, and here turning left first smelt the scent of woodsmoke, then found yourself at Middlebank door.

Only part of the house was habitable, but the Bowmans were happy with its position, the rent of one shilling a week with a lease from the farmer into the bargain. Sometimes the water supply worked, the rats were a trouble, wild bees made honey in the rafters, but the view of the wide Carse to the south, the Fife hills and waters of the Tay made all the inconveniences worthwhile. How wonderful it was in the snow-drifts of winter, and when spring bought forth white blossom, and when in summer you could hear cuckoos calling from the slopes of Black Law west beyond the upland pastures.

Now you must understand that Les was a heavy smoker, and like many such would give up the habit if he could. As a self-imposed discipline he cut down his smoking at the weekends, relying on a twenty pack to see him through Saturday and Sunday in a situation where the nearest shop was five miles away and he had no motor car. Many a Sunday night, therefore, Les was reduced to rummaging in old jackets looking for fags, and all but wrenching up floorboards in hopes of an odd Woodbine dropped during renovations.

It came over me one evening that I might try a surprise visit to Les and Betty, take a taxi to the check bar road end, and tap my way to the house, thus astonishing my friends with what would be nothing more or less than a virtuoso performance. So on a Sunday night in November I left the taxi, assuring the driver darkness meant nothing to me, and that in a bitter wind and four inches of untrodden snow I could find my way to the house. I could feel the ruts with my stick, hear the wind in the trees on my right and came at length to the stone parapet of the hump-backed bridge. I managed the right turn, found the left turn beyond, and here I had to be specially careful, for if I drifted through a certain opening by mistake, I would be irretrievably lost in the area known as the Piper Dam.

I managed the turn, and it was with rising confidence I felt my way to come abreast of the old dry stane dyke. I sniffed, and sure enough, there was the scent of woodsmoke on the breeze, the certainty that Middlebank with its stove and never cold teapot and hot buttered toast was just out of my grasp. It wasn't easy to find the door, but find it I did, raised my stick and knocked. What praise would be lavished on me, I thought, for this bold enterprise; what awe would be evinced in my indomitable fortitude, what incredulity that such a feat could be accomplished by a blind man, bearing in mind the terrain, the snow conditions, and the fact that I had never attempted it before.

The door opened. Les seized my arm. "Have you any fags ?" he said in a voice of desperation. It was only when I had satisfied him on this point that I was ushered into the warmth and companionship inside.

> By Middlebank I and the Bowmans mean
> Not what it is, but what it once became,
> Less house than half a legend, half a name.
> There Leslie, Betty and myself had seen
> Such beauty burst in whiteness on the gean
> As made most rare that cracked, time-tumbled frame
> Where once I loved to come, where much I came,
> Sharing a richness that had ruin been.

Those times have come and silent slipped away
Which memory now shapes within its hold;
Not ours alas, that Piper Dam today,
Where curlews cried and something far, far less
Than when it stoned our homeward steps of old
The Check Bar road turns into emptiness.

By 1946, when I went up as a blind undergraduate to New College, the city of dreaming spires had long since become the city of screaming tyres, but nevertheless much of its past still remained securely locked up in the quadrangles and cloisters of its numerous colleges. To these academic havens repaired many ex-servicemen in those days, not all of them British, and one who came to be a pal was an American, Charlie Apt, who was up on an army scholarship, reading nuclear physics. He was a sharp, energetic Brooklyn man, invariably cheerful, and when I asked him to describe a typical day in his laboratories, he made as I imagine a sensitive gesture: "They just hand you an atom as you go in the door, Scrog," he said "and tell you to get on with it."

The bell of New College clanged the hours, as it had done since 1376; an old bit of Saxon wall divided the two quadrangles; you could hear young choristers from the chapel nearby, and daily I put on my commoners gown, tapped my way to the foot of a certain stair, and had my tutorial on some aspect of history or other, under the greatest man it has ever been my fortune to know, David Ogg.

The Commandant of the G.H.Q. Battle School, Colonel Wigram, made a better soldier out of me than ever I could have managed myself. And now at New College this venerable Scotsman, a Fellow of the College, expanded my mind as far as it would go, teaching me to read and think. Sir Ian Fraser, the Chairman of St. Dunstan's, spoke a great truth when he said a blind man couldn't get too much education. David Ogg awoke what latent capacities I had, and they have stood me in good stead ever since. Oxford gave me so very much; rowing on the Isis with a friend at the tiller; recitals of chamber music; meeting with some very nice girls who read to me; blethering with fellow undergraduates, and savouring the sense of humour of David Ogg who gifted me with something worth an M.A. (Oxon) in itself - his book "Europe in the 17th century", with a letter inside it containing the words: "You were the best history student in your year."

Adaption to disability is simple, though it may take a little time to discover this. There are disabilities worse than blindness or deafness - mutilation or paralysis, for instance, embitterdness, which destroys not the body but the soul.

At St. Dunstan's I had learned how to work a telephone switchboard, and by reason of this I got a job in a Dundee factory, and worked there until I chose to retire in 1975. Two miles I walked up the road every morning, two miles down in the evening, and in the middle of the day I walked a further two miles to the Birkhill Inn where my mid-yoking consisted of a pie and a pint.

"Why," asked a pal of mine, Jim Hood, "do you walk up the Birkie Brae on the right hand side? There's no path there." My reply was that the path was in the shade and I wanted my shirt off in the sunshine. "That's all very well," said Jim, " but there's a terrible amount of cars on that road. Have you never had a fright ?" I said "No." Said Jim, "Well, according to various friends of mine, you should have had !"

My first marriage was to Barbara Elizabeth Ingram from Taunton in Somerset. She had been a nursing sister at St. Dunstan's, Ovingdean, and in her day, at the height of the London blitz, had drawn the ward curtains at Bartholomew Hospital to conceal from her patients the red glare of fires. When I brought her to her new home, Roseangle, Strathmartine, Angus, she noticed the sun was blue that afternoon and just shut the door on it. How Barbara saw it now was that she was in Scotland, and there might as often be blue suns as golden ones in the south.

I was getting back to the hills at this time, Corrour bothy, the Shelter Stone, Johnny Robertson's barn, Glen Muick, the Broadcairn hut; at the same time Jamie, Sydney and Mary had been born, and I owe a profound debt to Barbara that she never demurred from my being away from home at the weekends. She knew how important the hills were to me, though not perhaps understanding it, and showed neither noisy protestation nor silent disapproval. Barbara died in 1980, by which time I had some 500 trips to my credit, each noted down under "Heather, Bog and Boulder" as the log of these trips is entitled.

> Here is the start and here the end
> Of many a mountain day,
> And what do we buy that we should spend
> Our time this tinker way.
> We buy what never the fool shall please
> Nor over the knave have power,
> The things that are one with the wind and the trees
> And a fire at Altanour.

It has been with my wife Margaret, who is also my best pal, that I have spent more time in corrie and glen, on plateau and mountain top, much more than with anyone else. " I can do without my eyes," I am reported to have said at the outset of my blindness, "but I cannot do without my mountains." That this dilemma was resolved, I owe as much to Margaret, as to the many friends who have had me, whether in Clova or Muick, Geldie or Tilt, Taitneach or Ey, under their care.

I am an incomer here in Strathmartine, though of nearly 40 years standing; she is an aborigine; and from the time we first climbed Craigowl together - the local hill - there has been virtually no trip of mine in which she did not also take part. The hills are who you are with, and Corrour bothy would not have been the same for me; the Sinclair hut, the Shelter Stone, the Bourach, Glas Allt Sheil, Luibeg, the Black Burn bothy, Culra Lodge and Ben Alder cottage; had they not become, each in turn, places I shared with her. We have been on 70 or 80 Munros together, hundreds of sub-Munros, and it is not to be supposed that in the course of all these expeditions, we have not found ourselves in positions of danger.

We've had bad experiences in snow-squalls, and on frozen slopes without ice-axe and crampons, but it was on Carn a'Mhaim I came as near to death as I ever did amongst the Spandaus and Schmeissers, 88's and mortars of the Italian cam-

From Braeriach looking across to Carn a' Mhaim where Syd and Margaret had their dangerous fall

paign. And it was Margaret who saved my life. It was summer and having made our way to the top by a roundabout route, Margaret reconnoitred forward for a shorter way down to Corrour bothy.

"It's awfully steep," was her report, "But I think we might just get down." For me it meant sitting on my backside, and using boulders to ease myself down. Margaret's voice came up from below saying it continued steep like this as far as she could see. My weight was on a stone when it gave way, and down I went with it rolling over and over. I could do nothing to stop myself, felt my thigh hit a rock, collided with Margaret and sent her rolling down the slope as well. She fetched up against something which stopped her, and as I rolled past flung herself on me and brought me to a stop. I lost my pipe out of this, a new one, and there is nothing more certain that without that something that stopped Margaret, the two of us would have been killed, for the slope became vertical crag not fifty feet lower down. As I rolled down the slope I seemed to leave my body and take no more than a detached interest in what was happening to my physical frame. I was seeing the end of Sydney Scroggie. But when I bumped into Margaret I re-entered my body, became my old self again, and was able to comfort her when she burst into tears. We managed between us, but only just managed, to get up the slope again and go back down the hill by the way we had come.

Above the Black Spout, Lochnagar

In my rock climbing days before the War, John Ferguson had the brains and I the brawn. John, who was little more than a schoolboy, had taken a photograph of Lochnagar's north eastern corrie, enlarged it, and studying Eagle Buttress, saw the possibility of straightening out an old route and making a new one up it. So off we went with food for a week, carrying pitons, hammer and rope, to camp at the Spittal of Glen Muick, stars in the sky, a whiff of woodsmoke, and the glare of our fire reflecting from the pine branches.

Next day, camping in the bouldery corrie below the black crags, we went for Raeburn's Gully, finding its big chock stone a bit awkward, walked across the summit, then pottered our way down the Black Spout looking for gemstones among the shattered screes. Below us was the little loch, and in the fading light the croak of a ptarmigan sounded, echoing from crag to crag.

It rained and blew next day, the mist was down to the tent, but mid-day saw John and I well up the new line that John had picked out. Wet through we sat snugly belayed on a little ledge, Douglas Gully on one side, Parallel Gully A on the other, and above our heads, dimly visible in the mist, bulging rock challenging us to find a way, if we could summon up enough nerve.

It meant a long step right to a good hold, then an upward pull round into a scoop. Safeguarded by John I got my right foot on the hold, made a hard move, reached up and found not one hold in the scoop but two. There was no way back. My right foot taking my weight began to shake; I sprang upwards to jam my knees against the enclosing walls. It enabled me to hammer a piton into a crack, slip my rope into it and shout to John to take the strain and let me abseil off.

Given better weather we might have made the first ascent of Eagle Ridge, one of the great classics of Lochnagar. We failed at its crux. What I got out of that day however was something vouchsafed to few in any field of activity, a truly supreme moment when capacity was pushed to its limit and mortal danger threatened. There were to be other moments like it. The only thing that compares to such moments in rock climbing is the exhilaration of battle in war against an enemy.

I write about some things that are no more. The Glen Doll hut fell down at last. The Broadcairn hut got blown away, preserving to the end, however, a pencilled message on its old plank walls: "3rd October, 1937. C. Brand, J. Scroggie, Scroggie" this in commemoration of what was my very first trip with my brother Jack into the hills. This book recalls focal points and focal people of innumerable excursions, a conjuring of the snows of winter, the heat of summer and the rain at all times in such a rhapsody of hill situations that I envy no other man his.

"If you're daft enough to want to go the hills Scroggie, then I'm daft enough to want to go with you." It was Bob McLean speaking. Then there was Bill Dye, Denny Fagan, Gavin Sprott and Barabbas, Ronnie McCabe, Martin Pirie, Ian Petrie, Judith Good and Patricia Tierney, George Shanks, my cousin Donald Bewick, Margaret, Mary, Jamie and Sydney Scroggie; had they not all of them been daft enough to come with me I could not have got the length of Dundee Law, never mind Blaven Macdhui, Carn nan Gabhar and Ben Nevis.

I am 70 now, but am dubbining my boots, Margaret's as well, for what could be, for all anyone knows, my last look around from Morrone or Glas Maol, my last sniff at the wind that blows in the wilderness.

I will attempt the Capel Track,
Old, stiff and retrograde,
And set some pal to push me on
Should resolution fade.
For I must see black Meikle Pap
Against a starry sky,
And watch the dawn from Lochnagar
Once more before I die.

The golden plover whistled there
Before the fall of man,
And you can hear the brittle croak
Of lonely ptarmigan.
No heather there, but boulders bare
And quartz and granite grit
And ribs of snow, bleak, old and grey
As I remember it.
And if I do not make the top
Then sit me on a stone,
Some lichen'd rock amongst the screes,
And leave me there alone.
Yes, leave me there alone to hear,
Where spout, and buttress are,
The breeze that stirs the little loch
On silent Lochnagar.

7th December.
Roseangle
Kirkton of Strathmartine,
by Dundee, Angus.